Disclaimer: The opinions presented herein are solely those of the author except where specifically noted. Nothing in the book should be construed as advice or guidance, as it is not intended as advice or guidance, nor is it offered as such. Nothing in the book should be construed as a recommendation to buy or sell any financial or physical asset. It is solely the opinion of the writer, who is not an investment professional. The publisher/author disclaims any implied warranty or applicability of the contents for any particular purpose. The publisher/author shall not be liable for any commercial or incidental damages of any kind or nature.

First edition published April 2022

Oftwominds.com
P.O. Box 10847
Hilo HI 96721

Cover: Theresa Barzyk

With gratitude to my companion in burnout C.N.F. for her insights and editing—we understand each other in ways no one else can.

When You Can't Go On:
Burnout, Reckoning and Renewal

Charles Hugh Smith

Table of Contents

Introduction

I've burned out twice, once in my early 30s and again in my mid-60s. What I wanted but could not find was a practical guide by someone who had experienced burnout themselves. In the mid-1980s, there were few resources. When I burned out again in 2018, there were numerous books and articles, but none spoke to my feeling that burnout was more than overwork, or to my sense that our society and economy are the kindling that ignites burnout.

I decided to write the guide I wanted but could not find, a guide to burnout as an intensely profound experience, an experience those who haven't burned out cannot fully understand.

You may find that my experience is different from yours; this is to be expected, for burnout differs with individuals, circumstances and age. What's universal about burnout is that it is a gift of life, an opportunity to look deep within ourselves and an opportunity to change. In the depths of exhaustion, despair and depression, it feels like a curse. But the more profound the gift, the greater the difficulty in understanding and making use of it.

The story about the desert traveler who comes across a hoard of gold coins comes to mind. To maximize the amount of gold to be carried away, the traveler dumps the food and water from his pack and sets off, empowered by the shimmering dreams of all the luxuries and status the gold would buy. Long before reaching the glittering bazaar where gold reigns supreme, the traveler realizes the real treasure was the water and food that he foolishly dumped, for his life depended not on gold but on what he had tossed away.

This book is organized to first offer a hand to hold for those experiencing burnout: you are not alone; I've been in the same place and got through it. So have many others. There are no miracle quick cures (at least to my knowledge), but perhaps reading about my experiences may help in small ways. Over time, small things add up and we feel better.

The second part is intended to help those who want to explore the sources and lessons of burnout. Burnout is a life-changing experience, in a good way, as absurd as that sounds to those in the depths of burnout.

This is my personal account of burnout. I am not a therapist, psychologist, psychiatrist or physician. Those professionals can all provide help; that's what they are trained to do. This is not an expert's clinical guide to burnout, or a survey of the literature on burnout. It is not intended as advice or guidance. I am simply sharing one individual's experience of burnout, reckoning and renewal, and what helped me.

Chapter One: My Experience of Burnout

Before we begin: *Please remember I am not an expert in burnout, I am only an expert in my own burnout. This is not advice or guidance. I am only sharing my experience, which might not be relevant to your experience or useful to anyone else. It's very important to me that you keep in mind that I am only sharing my experience and views.*

I like working, and I like my work. That wasn't the problem.

The problem was I didn't think I had any limits. I thought that I could keep pushing myself even as I became increasingly exhausted.

But all humans have limits. Mine were not visible to me. Even as I slipped closer and closer to my limits, I did not see the cliff edge just ahead. When I exceeded my limits, I burned out.

Burnout teaches us we all have limits.

What is burnout? In my experience, when our capacity to keep working drops to zero, that's burnout. We want to continue working, but the capacity to do so is no longer in our control. We hit our limit, and there's no fuel left in our tank.

We want the validation, purpose and livelihood we gained from work but we can no longer do the work. This loss of power and control is distressing and puzzling. Why is this happening to me?

Here's what I felt at the bottom of burnout: an exhaustion deeper than I'd ever felt before, a tiredness that never ended, a collapse of my willpower and a depression that never lifted.

I lost the self-discipline that that I'd maintained without much difficulty for years. I also lost the *joie de vivre*, the joy of being alive, which had been replaced by exhaustion and a feeling of unending stress: I'll never get out from beneath terrible burdens and never catch up or be free from crushing responsibilities.

Though I didn't want to admit it, I also felt self-pity: I'm trapped, hopeless, and misunderstood.

Even my spouse, who would burn out six months later, made light of my exhaustion, dismissing it as temporary and mere complaints.

Only those who have fallen down the same well can understand, and I didn't have any other burnouts to consult. That's one of the things that makes burnout so painful: the burnout is often totally alone.

Those of us who are accustomed to accomplishing a great deal and being in charge are most devastated by burnout because we pride ourselves on being productive and take-charge.

Our willpower and ability to work hard are lost in burnout: we can no longer force ourselves to take charge, and since burnout is outside of our control, we feel a devastating powerlessness.

Burnout is the loss of self. Our trusted tools no longer work; something in our life is broken, and it's broken us.

Burnout isn't something you choose, it's something that happens to you against your will. Willing it to go away doesn't make it go away.

Burnout is frustrating not just because it's outside our control; it's also beyond our understanding of how the world works. We rely on our intellect, experience and willpower to solve problems, and all three come up empty in burnout: we don't know how to make burnout go away, our previous experience doesn't apply and our will—our most trusted tool in managing the world—has collapsed.

We're completely broken There's nothing left in our tank: no reserves, no willpower, no control of what's happening to us. We haven't just lost our energy; we've lost our sense of who we are.

Being positive is the secular religion of America: the power of a positive attitude can solve any problem and overcome any obstacle. This is the can-do spirit: if you stop being negative, you'll become a winner.

The problem for the burnout is there is nothing left to fuel a can-do attitude, and so revealing the despair we feel draws criticism: stop being so negative, here's a self-help checklist, follow this and you'll be back on your feet in no time.

Being positive has a dual nature. Much of the positivity we hear is phony because it's for public consumption: never mind what you actually feel, just repeat the positive script aloud because that's what makes everyone comfortable.

Burnouts who are unable to repeat the positive script with the expected enthusiasm become castaways; not only does no one understand our distress, we're criticized for not being upbeat.

The implicit message is: you could fix your burnout if you'd just be more positive. Your stress will melt away once you say positive things. But the unending stress doesn't melt away—it melts us away.

The non-burned-out haven't felt so drained that there's nothing left to prop up the expected cheerfulness. With no experience of burnout, they cannot understand the gravity of what we're feeling.

The burnout soon gives up expressing what we're experiencing rather than bear the additional burden of criticism.

This disapproval further isolates the burnout; nobody wants to hear how the burnout feels because that makes everyone uncomfortable.

Whether we want to admit it or not—usually not until much later in the process—burnout is a life-changing experience. This further isolates the burnout because everyone wants us to bounce back and resume the work we did before we collapsed. But the burnout can't do the same work. Going back isn't possible, and nobody wants to hear that.

This inability to return to the harness—and a growing unwillingness to do so—runs counter to the kind of self-help counseling which focuses on helping the burnout strap themselves back into overwork and open-ended responsibility. To reject this is unacceptable to everyone who depended on the burnout being an uncomplaining pack animal.

Burnouts find the world is dead-set on our prompt return to the workload that broke us. The self-help industry is typically focused on helping the pack animal stagger back to its feet because this what our economy depends on: work hard, play hard and strive for achievement, wealth and recognition. Anything less and the economy unravels.

Whether those still have any meaning is not a question anyone other than the burnout wants to ask, as the question challenges their assumptions about what's meaningful and worthy of sacrifice.

The end result is the burnout is alone. Not only does no one understand us, no one wants to understand we won't be resuming our workload.

What the non-burned-out don't understand is the burnout has been so drained there is nothing left. Rewards for our work have vanished, along with the means to carry heavy burdens. The pack animal has collapsed and cannot get to its feet, no matter how many people flog it.

The messages the burnout hears are not helpful. Some might begin as superficially sympathetic, but only as an introduction to *try harder to not be burned out*, even though trying harder is what burned us out.

Everyone is worried because they're not prepared to do everything we can no longer do. They can't help wanting us to get better so we can go back to making their lives easier.

The burnout is annoyed, to the degree we can feel anything at all, because it's now clear that nobody really cares about our well-being. They care about whatever we kept glued together: the enterprise, the household, and the facade of normalcy and cheerfulness.

The burnout no longer cares about any of that because we no longer have the means to care. The burnout may want to care, may feel pressure to care, but neither gives us the means to care.

The tank is bone-dry and so no matter how much the burnout wants to care, we no longer have the energy to care.

The burnout understands others depend on us, and so we feel guilty for being burned out. The burnout understands that others fear the collapse of their own lives should we fail to get back on our feet.

But we cannot help but have mixed feelings that our health matters less than our work. Advice to take a week off, drink fresh lemon juice, take supplements, etc., as if overwork and not taking care of ourselves were easily fixable with superficial cures, isn't helpful.

The burnout never feels more alone than when hearing yet another suggestion to take a few days off, listen to calming music, treat yourself to some luxury, etc., for superficial to-do lists only increase the distance between the castaway and the shore left behind.

Your experience of burnout may have been less difficult. Perhaps you had supportive, understanding people around you who had no stake in whatever collapsed in the wake of your burnout. Others haven't been so blessed.

Dreams are one of the few reliable sources of insight available to the burnout. One of my dreams offers a vivid summary of the burnout's dilemma.

In the dream, I parked my car and crossed a dry creek bed on foot to reach a remote construction site. Unable to locate the site, I retraced my steps and found the creek had become a raging river I could not possibly ford. At that point I realized I'd left my phone in my car. I was stranded and unable to contact anyone.

That's the burnout's dilemma: unable to return to our previous life, unable to communicate with others and unable to find a new beginning.

To paraphrase Samuel Beckett: I can't go on but I must go on.

(Beckett's line was "You must go on. I can't go on. I'll go on.")

Burnout isn't a destination we choose to visit and leave. it's a reckoning no one chooses, a forced quest of discovery, and so we must go on even though we're broken. Although there is no path visible ahead, there is a way forward.

Chapter Two: Triage

Nobody knows what will be most helpful to someone else in the depths of burnout; I certainly don't. I do know that if a weekend getaway and a shopping spree resolve your exhaustion, you aren't burned out. If you're burned out, planning a getaway is a joyless burden, never mind getting to the hideaway, and shopping is just another ordeal.

I titled this chapter *Triage* to introduce the idea that the goal is to *stop the bleeding and start the healing*. Burnouts aren't bleeding from open wounds, but we're wounded physically and psychologically nonetheless.

Triage is the process of prioritizing care to those most in need. The burnout is the person most in need, so we must start caring for ourselves. The goal is to reduce whatever is causing burnout so it doesn't get worse and take the first steps toward healing ourselves.

We can't help anyone else unless we first help ourselves.

Get Help

Let's start with the obvious: if you need help, get help. In my first burnout at age 33, I became very depressed and sought the help of a psychiatrist. I chose to see a medical doctor (psychiatrists are MDs) because I wanted someone who looked at the entirety of my health, not just my depression.

In my second burnout at age 63, I consulted my doctor (*primary care physician*) and asked for a battery of tests to confirm the burnout hadn't damaged my health, and to check if some unknown medical issue might have triggered my burnout. Fortunately, the test results were normal. But it was certainly prudent to check and prudent to seek help. Exhaustion has many possible sources, including Myalgic Encephalomyelitis/chronic fatigue syndrome (ME/CFS).

As the visibility of burnout increases, the number of professionals with experience helping burnouts has also increased. Not all physicians and mental health professionals have experience treating burnout.

The psychiatrist my spouse consulted after she burned out gave her a prescription for an anti-depressant and sent her on her way without asking about the life circumstances causing her depression. It may require a search to find professionals with experience treating burnout.

Research has found (*Scientific American*, January 2022, *The Long Shadow of Trauma*) that having someone with whom we can share our experiences, is the key difference between those who struggle with the aftermath of trauma and those who manage to have fulfilling lives despite traumatic experiences. As one researcher put it: "Of course, it's unpleasant, it's a disaster. But it's not so disastrous if you can share it."

It's not helpful to suffer in silence, so finding someone with whom you can share your experience is an important step toward healing.

How Long Will It Take to Get Through This?

It's natural to ask, "when will it end?" because we're suffering and so we hope burnout will end soon. In the depths of her burnout, my spouse sought answers to the question "how long will it last?" in others' experiences.

There is no one-size-fits-all answer. Some burnouts report being back to normal in a few months while others report still being burned out a year later.

No one can say how long it will take to emerge from burnout because it depends on the individual's circumstance and age, and whether the sources of burnout are identified and reduced or eliminated.

In my experience, it's not helpful to focus on speeding up the process. Just as it took a long time to burn out, it may take an equivalent period of time to work through the reckoning and the renewal.

Burning out and recovering from burnout are both imperceptible as they're happening. It's a process of small steps that can't be leapfrogged or hurried.

It's akin to watching a deep cut heal. You want it to heal immediately, but this can't happen as you wish. The wound heals in its own time, without you noticing it until you notice the pain is gone and it's healed.

Burnout is like this. You'll notice when you feel better, but expecting rapid healing is frustrating. Healing proceeds on its own time.

Trying to get through burnout as fast as possible as if the recovery were a task that can be accelerated by sheer will is what burned us out in the first place.

One of the lessons of burnout is that we're not in absolute control of the recovery process any more than we were in absolute control of our slide into burnout.

If we'd had total control of everything, we wouldn't have burned out in the first place.

Our mind and body are one, but each operates at its own pace. Our mind may desire to push us to get through burnout in a set length of time, as if the recovery was just another deadline to meet. But our body doesn't respond to the mind's manic deadlines; the body will heal itself in its own time, not according to the mind's schedule.

Our emotional health recovers on its own pace, too, and can't be hurried.

Our burnout-impaired intellectual capabilities also take their own time to recover. My memory, ability to focus and my overall judgement were all impaired by burnout. It took a long time for me to regain my pre-burnout capabilities.

Burnout teaches us to become patient. I am an impatient person and so learning this was difficult. But there really isn't a choice, as becoming frustrated and anxious about the speed of one's recovery only adds stress that further delays recovery.

Rather than focus on trying to hurry what cannot be hurried, we serve our best interests by focusing in making progress one step at a time. Making small improvements is what we do control,

My view is that burnout is life-changing experience. It is not a destination you visit and then return from unchanged. Four years after hitting bottom, I am still learning about my post-burnout self and life. I say more about this in the section *Where we are now*.

Make a Simple Recovery Plan

The mind and body have evolved to heal themselves. We can either help or hinder this healing.

Just as the mind is accustomed to setting deadlines and goals, it's also accustomed to making demanding plans to reach the goal faster.

Complicated plans require more energy than we can muster. Make a simple plan that we can follow every day even though we're exhausted.

There is no instant cure to burnout. Just as the slide into burnout was imperceptible, progress out of burnout is also imperceptible. Over time, small efforts that aid our healing accumulate, much like a spring will fill a pond one drop at a time.

R. Buckminster Fuller famously described how one individual can change the course of an entire society. His analogy is the *trim tab*, which he described as "...a miniature rudder. Just moving the little trim tab builds a low pressure that pulls the rudder around. Takes almost no effort at all. So I said that the little individual can be a trim tab."

In other words, making a small adjustment in the trim tab will eventually change the course of a mighty ship.

The small adjustments we make can be thought of as trim tabs: taking a walk, rewarding ourselves for completing any task, no matter how small, and learning replacement thoughts for those that generate despair. These small changes eventually change the course of our life.

What worked for me was focusing on one small task even though I did not feel up to it: prepare a simple meal, answer an email, etc.

The goal of a simple recovery plan is to put Fuller's insight about small adjustments into a stripped-down daily list that an utterly exhausted burnout can manage.

In my experience, what's pervasive in burnout is the feeling of an endless exhaustion only rest and sleep can heal.

What worked for me was listening to my own body rather than trying to follow a rigid schedule, rest and sleep as my body dictated.

In my experience, our emotional health also needs time to heal. I needed time alone. I had no energy for socializing or even answering the phone. I needed all my limited energy to get through the day and follow my simple recovery plan.

As I keep saying, I am not an expert on burnout, I am only an expert on my burnout. I don't know what will help anyone else; I can only share what helped me. Here is my simple recovery plan.

1. Eat healthy food.

2. Personal care.

3. Light exercise.

4. Write down dreams, thoughts and feelings.

5. Give myself credit for completing a task.

6. Rest and sleep.

The list is simple cause and effect. We can either help or hinder our recovery. Our daily actions, no matter how small, steer the ship of our recovery and our life.

Eating healthy food, light exercise and positive habits aid our healing. Junk food, being sedentary and self-medication hinder healing. Helping and hindering are cause and effect: depriving ourselves of real food, exercise and healing habits has negative consequences. Treating ourselves well by eating real food and forging habits of exercise and healthy mental health practices has positive consequences.

1. What is a nutritious diet? There are endless cultural and individual variations, but they all boil down to real food: fresh fruits and vegetables, whole grains and legumes, and wholesomely raised or wild fish and meat. Processed food has little or no role in a healthy diet.

I wish I'd kept a diary of our menu when we were both burned out. I forget the details but we managed to prepare simple, healthy meals.

 That there were three cooks in the house was a big plus: my elderly Mom-in-law, my spouse and I all prepared meals. As long as one of us scraped up the energy to go shopping or make a meal, we all benefited.

What worked for us was to plan a few days' meals so we'd have wholesome food on hand: fresh fruit and vegetables, dried beans, etc. We favored one-dish meals such as stir-fry that offered variety.

Meal prep is a challenge for burnouts who live alone, but there are workarounds: stews, soups and dishes that offer leftovers or extra portions to freeze, etc.

Our mind/body are designed to heal themselves, but we need to provide nutritious fuel for that healing.

2. When we feel so exhausted, it's tempting to let go of personal care habits such as taking a shower, washing your hair, brushing your teeth and getting dressed for the day. In my experience, maintaining our basic personal-care routine makes us feel better and is part of healing.

3. Walk every day. Walking is our natural curative, our natural state of motion. Walking stimulates positive dynamics in our body and our mind. Even when we were exhausted, we walked every day, even if it was a short walk. (If not a walk, a light exercise equivalent.)

We explored our neighborhood to find routes that offered some natural beauty, for walking and Nature are healing.

4. Write down your thoughts, insights and dreams every day, even if you don't feel that it's helping. Writing down what we're thinking, feeling and dreaming is essential, as we may not remember our dreams and thoughts from a few days ago. Writing them down engages our focus and allows us to re-read what we wrote later. In my experience, this is an essential step in the process of understanding and insight.

5. If you're like many other burnouts, you were accustomed to getting a lot done every day but rarely gave yourself credit for your productivity, attention to detail, accountability and service to others. Let's say you accomplished 100 points but gave yourself credit for only 10 points. You (and everyone around you) took your work for granted. Many of us only acknowledged what we could have done better and gave ourselves little credit for what we accomplished.

Credit yourself for every small task completed: changing bedsheets, doing laundry, washing dishes—they're all positive accomplishments.

Once we burn out, this ratio must be reversed. If we accomplish 10 points, we must give ourselves 100 points of credit because every task is arduous. We must acknowledge our effort, for now we need our own encouragement above all else. We cannot rely on others to praise what to them looks very modest indeed. Only the burnout understands that completing any task is now major accomplishment.

It took me every bit of willpower to get off the sofa and get something done. Giving myself credit for completing a task no matter how small improved my spirits and encouraged me to do so the next day.

 6. In my experience, it takes time to recover from extreme exhaustion, maybe much longer than we anticipate. Our conscious mind may have unrealistic expectations as it is not as exhausted as our body.

Exhaustion can disturb our sleep routine, leading to insomnia. It may be tempting to draw the curtains, close the bedroom door and stay in bed all day, as all we want is to be undisturbed and unstressed.

The downside of doing so is revealed by the difficulty in falling asleep at night. Any benefit gained by staying in bed all day is cancelled by the additional exhaustion and frustration of insomnia. Keeping daily routines helps maintain healthy sleep routines.

We aid our body's recovery by listening to its needs for rest and sleep, along with healthy food, moderate exercise, healing routines, self-encouragement and patience.

What Helped Me

No one knows what will help another individual, but we can share what helped us. Keeping these principles in mind helped me.

1. Burnout is like the governor on an engine that's running at top speed. As it overheats, the danger of the engine self-destructing rises. The governor shuts the engine down to protect it from self-inflicted damage. Burnout is the automatic safety valve that shuts us down before we self-destruct.

In other words, burnout protects us from harm. Though it may not feel like it, burnout is saving us.

2. America's can-do philosophy holds that all problems have solutions and anything is possible if we embrace the idea that there are *no limits*. The upside of this can-do spirit is inspirational, but glorifying *no limits* convinced us that each individual has no limits.

This dogma is a prescription for burnout, as we each have limits. Trying to live as if we have no limits self-creates burnout. Accepting that we all have limits is a necessary step to recovery.

3. Burnout reduces the energy available to spend on guilt, regret and anxiety about the future. I only have enough energy to deal with this hour and this day. Regret, guilt and worry all consume energy I no longer have to spare.

4. It's easy to label burnout a failure, but this isn't an accurate assessment. Burnout is a *reckoning*: whatever is no longer working in our lives wears us down and breaks us. Since we like to think of ourselves as strong, smart, competent and successful, losing those attributes feels like a failure. But it's not a failure, it's simply cause and effect in action: we exceeded our limits and burned out.

It was helpful to me to stop labeling burnout as a failure. Burnout happens despite our best efforts to keep going. Burnout is not a random bolt from the blue; it happens for a reason: stressors pile up and eventually break us. Once we understand it as cause and effect, then we can identify and address the causes.

5. It's easy to think "something's wrong with me." This is not a realistic assessment. Burnout is the result of sweeping what wasn't working under the carpet for everyone's sake, including our own.

What's deficient is our understanding of how we pushed ourselves over our limit and triggered the automatic shutoff of burnout.

6. Our expectations of ourselves were unrealistic. We thought the most important thing was to meet everyone's expectations and fulfill our own definition of success.

We tried to meet unrealistic demands of others and ourselves: to be near-perfect in our work, godlike in our strength and Zenlike in our resolve, wise beyond our years, never failing to make the right decision.

No one can meet these unrealistic demands, but we tend to forget that, and so instead of being a friend to ourselves we're our own harsh critic. Rather than being critical of ourselves, we must be mindful of the positives that still exist despite our burnout.

7. We need to be as good a friend to ourselves as we are to others. Just as we wouldn't endlessly criticize a friend, we shouldn't endlessly criticize ourselves, especially when we're struggling with burnout.

8. Changing distorted thoughts that lead to depression. After my first burnout at age 33, I became very depressed and consulted psychiatrist Dr. Mary Deluca. After five hectic, stressful years as a builder, I felt like a failure. My partner and I built dozens of houses, a 43-unit subdivision and a commercial/retail project but earned nothing but a modest wage.

Financially, the business was not a success: we'd both made so many sacrifices and poured in so much effort just to pay all our bills and earn the same wage we paid our foremen.

Spending five years running a business that burned me out felt like a failure. I loved the hands-on building but was worn down by the business and financial burdens and managing multiple crews.

The financial stress only increased as we expanded. The more we built, the more money we had to front. Neither of us was rich, so went without paychecks to pay our crews and subcontractors.

One thing I learned in therapy was a depressed person erases all the positives of their work and life and focuses exclusively on their mistakes, flaws, failures, regrets and poor prospects.

This is a gross distortion of reality. A realistic assessment acknowledges the positives of our work and life and credits us for what we accomplished. Dr. Deluca pointed out that we'd built affordable homes, employed many people and learned so much in a few years.

I learned to substitute these more realistic assessments for the gross distortions that pushed me down the chute into depression.

8. One way to incorporate these principles into every day is to write down all the helpful things we tend to forget and read them every day—or better yet, read them aloud every day. I call them *helpful things to keep in mind*. Here is my list. Reading it daily helped me.

-- I am a friend to myself.

-- Distorted thoughts are habits that can be changed. Distorted thoughts are not realistic. They create negative emotions. I replace unrealistic distorted thoughts with realistic assessments.

-- I am a positive person.

-- I am letting go of "*shoulds.*" I no longer need to do or be anything to be worthy. I am worthy as I am, i.e., burned out.

-- No one can be everything to everybody. If I lose myself, I have nothing to give others. My first responsibility is to regain my health. Only then will I be able to help others.

-- I have earned this period of reflection and exploration.

-- Feeling guilty because I'm burned out is not helpful. It doesn't help me or anyone else.

-- Focus on now, today. That is all we control.

Again, these are not suggestions for anyone else; these are things to keep in mind that helped me.

When we feel exhausted, it's difficult to do much of anything. But it is possible to eat very simple real food, take a short walk and write down a few of our thoughts. The mind and body are one, and like all of Nature, manifest cause and effect.

We cannot extinguish burnout with magic or a pill, but we can help our mind-body's own healing with daily effort on our own behalf.

Once we feel better, the goal is to eliminate sources of burnout so we can regain our capacity to enjoy life, do good work and help those we care about.

Chapter Three: Why We Burn Out

University of California-Berkeley professor Christina Malasch pioneered research on work situations that accelerate burnout. Her six-point list explains how a "normal" 40-hour a week job can burn us out:

1. An overwhelming workload

2. A loss of control

3. Not being rewarded for efforts

4. Not being part of a thriving community

5. Not being treated fairly

6. Having to adhere to the wrong values

I found it helpful to rephrase the list into these questions:

1. Is the workload sustainable?

2. Does the worker have choice and control over their work?

3. Does the worker receive recognition and rewards aligned to their output?

4. Is the workplace a supportive community?

5. Does the workplace foster fairness and respect for every worker?

6. Are there clear values guiding meaningful work?

If all these factors are negative, then a "normal" 40-hour a week job is more than enough to burn us out. If our workload is unsustainable, our responsibilities open-ended, our control over our work limited, we don't receive recognition and rewards commensurate with what we accomplish, our work environment is not supportive or fair and our work is no longer meaningful, this generates chronic stress that tears down our body, mind and spirit.

These also define our life beyond work; if these factors are negative in our relationships and household, the result is chronic stress.

While these factors are certainly consequential, I don't think they exhaust the causes of burnout.

Although the conventional view is that burnout is the result of overwork, this overlooks the great complexity of life outside work.

Work can be the least stressful part of one's life, a refuge from truly toxic sources of anxiety.

Although it may be obvious, certain personality types are prone to burning out while others are less likely to burn out.

The ambitious, driven, goal-oriented, perfectionist "Type A" personality is prone to burning out, while the laid-back, less ambitious person with lower expectations is far less likely to burn out.

In my view, a factor that few mention is the lower-expectations person may be comfortable with themselves as they are, while the driven perfectionist may subconsciously feel their "real self" is unworthy and so they strive for an "ideal self" who is worthy of recognition.

Children who grow up in households where the adults are too distracted by their own problems to validate the child's feelings, needs and interests, and encourage the child's development, are prone to feeling insecure.

Since the parents are incapable of providing the love and nurturing every child wants, the child naturally feels they are unworthy of being cherished. This feels terrible so the child naturally thinks that if they can somehow project a "better" version of themselves, they'll be worthy of the affection and validation they don't get at home.

This drive to project an *ideal self* who is worthy of recognition becomes the template of their lives.

Rather than accept the "real self's" insecure fears of being unworthy, the uncherished child devotes themselves to being recognized by making a splash in whatever way they can: acting out, becoming the class clown, developing an athletic, academic or artistic skill, being especially helpful to others, etc.

The mechanism for gaining self-worth may differ but the goal is the same: develop some way to gain the attention and praise of others.

Failure in whatever way we've chosen to become worthy is a deeply wounding failure of the "better self" who took the place of the "real self" who was emotionally abandoned, abused or simply ignored.

No wonder we're driven to project a persona that's worthy of the attention and validation we didn't get as a child.

But constantly projecting this "better self" is exhausting, and so the driven person burns out.

Alternatively, the driven person succeeds in becoming recognized, and then discovers their victory is hollow. Being adored by others doesn't actually grant us inner security. We're still nagged by a feeling that deep down, we're still unworthy.

In my experience, burnout isn't simply overwork that can be cured by taking a few weeks off. It's a life crisis that compels us to look at issues deeper than overwork.

Burnout is the result of being done with a livelihood, a circumstance, and the self we present to the world. Perhaps we had to burn out because only then could we learn something important that we couldn't learn any other way.

In my view, *burnout is an involuntary intolerance for what no longer works in our lives*. Burnout is a reckoning and an opportunity for renewal, a gift that can be rejected or accepted. If we reject it, we will continue burning out. If we accept the gift, we gain a new worldview and a new appreciation of ourselves.

Chapter Four: Burnout's Hidden Complexities: It's Not Just Work

To truly heal burnout, we need to identify the sources of burnout. If we only address the symptoms but not the sources, we will continue to be burned out. These are sources I've identified as relevant to my burnout. They may not be relevant to your burnout.

What Healthcare Misses

In my experience, the chronic stress that leads to burnout has two sources: causes within *the individual* and causes within our *socio-economic system*. What makes us a unique individual--our personality, values and experience—is the conventional focus of healthcare.

This therapeutic focus on illnesses to be cured and symptoms to be alleviated is a major industry. Healthcare is almost 20% of the America economy. Trillions of dollars support treating illnesses and symptoms. From this perspective, burnout is a condition that can be treated with conventional means: medications to relieve insomnia, depression and anxiety, and therapies to aid recovery so burnouts can return to work.

The possibility that it's not just the individual's situation that is the source of burnout but our socio-economic system does not compute within the healthcare system. The only response to a socio-economic system that burns people out is to help individuals cope with burnout.

If the source of burnout is the socio-economic system, the healthcare system has no means to address this source. If the burnout says, "my job is killing me, I can't do it anymore," the response is "here are some pills to alleviate your symptoms, and here are self-help techniques to help you find another job and get back to work."

The healthcare industry isn't going to say, "the socio-economic system burns us out, the only way to heal yourself is to leave the system."

There is no industry that focuses on helping individuals deal with socio-economic sources of burnout.

These causes are poorly understood because they are outside conventional economics and healthcare. Economics focuses on measuring money, interest rates, etc. It has no interest in measuring burnout, which is far more difficult to measure than money.

The healthcare industry recognizes chronic stress, but it doesn't recognize the socio-economic system as the source of stress. It only recognizes "this job is stressful for this individual." The solution offered is to find a less stressful job or make time for a hobby. The healthcare system isn't designed to say, "the source of your burnout is our socio-economic system."

There are no conventional measures of these sources of burnout. Just because we don't measure these sources of burnout doesn't mean they don't exist. They are very real and devastating for individuals.

The Economy 's Role in Burnout

The nature of work has changed in ways that wear us down. Those who profit from our work aren't interested in reducing the workload because that would reduce profits.

There are two reasons we don't recognize social-economic sources of burnout. One is that burnout doesn't fit neatly into any existing category. Economics looks at individuals as rational beings who calculate what's in their best financial interests and respond to incentives such as higher pay.

That our economic system burns out its workers doesn't compute. There is no space in economics for the idea that the economy diminishes and sickens us.

Healthcare seeks causes of illness. Is burnout a conventional illness? Is it caused by genetic flaws, viruses, bacteria, or an unhealthy diet, i.e., a *lifestyle disease*? Burnout has characteristics of illness but it can't be fully understood as a disease with biological causes. Its symptoms also defy easy categorization.

Is it just exhaustion? If it were just exhaustion, rest would cure it. But rest doesn't cure burnout. If it's not just exhaustion, then what is it?

The other reason these sources of burnout are ignored is that they are extremely inconvenient for the status quo. What will happen if people recognize the system is burning them out and the only solution is to minimize participation in the system? Who will do the work that generates profits and tax revenues?

If the system burns out workers, how can this be the best possible economic system? Do we all benefit equally from this system, or do the few benefit at the expense of the many? What would an economy that didn't burn people out look like? These questions challenge those who benefit most from it, so these questions only arise on the fringes.

For simplicity's sake, let's say that individual circumstances are half the source of burnout and the socio-economic system is the source of the other half.

This means that modifying our individual circumstances cannot eliminate all the sources of burnout. We can't change everything in our circumstances—our upbringing, experiences and personality—nor can we change the economic system. This means to cure burnout we have to limit our participation in the system.

Our Individual Complexities

Our individual circumstances are complicated and many parts are hidden. For example, we say we like things when we actually don't like them because saying we like them is easier than causing conflicts or alienating others. We say we're happy when we're not happy for the same reasons.

We think we should know what we like and what makes us happy but we can't find the answers until we ask ourselves these questions directly. The answers may not be as easy to find as we expect.

Taking a pill will not reveal the parts of our lives that are hidden. The healthcare industry relies on pharmacological treatments of symptoms such as anxiety and depression. There is little effort devoted to exploring the hidden parts of ourselves that may be sources of burnout.

Time is money and insurers won't pay for much of the can't-be-hurried process of discovering what might be causing our burnout.

In my experience, there are three layers in ourselves which can each contribute to burnout.

The first is the complicated nature of human thoughts and emotions which we all share.

Our minds seek patterns and stories which explain why things happen, and these help us understand the past and anticipate the future.

Our minds are drawn to analogies as ways to understand things. For example, it's been popular to view the human mind as a biological computer. We can add a column of numbers, a computer can add a column of numbers, and so our minds and computers are similar.

But our minds are not computers. The human mind is tied in still-mysterious ways to our bodies. When we're given a pill and told it will make our pain go away, the pain may go away: the pill worked. But the pill was just sugar; it contained no medication. Our belief that the pill would work generated the positive result. This is called the placebo effect. Our beliefs can achieve miraculous results.

The brain is intimately connected to our digestive system, the gut. When we say we have a gut feeling, this is not just a saying. Scientists are far from understanding these deep connections between our digestive system (the microbiome) and our psychological well-being.

The human mind must dream to function properly. Deprived of sleep and dreaming, humans no longer function. Dreaming is still mysterious, and may well be inherently mysterious.

We are not conscious of these processes and connections. They occur independent of our conscious awareness.

The second layer is our conscious awareness and abilities—our ability to focus on a task, to learn something new, and so on. These unconscious and conscious processes often conflict.

For example, we feel hungry and this distracts us from whatever we're doing. If we're alone, we make time for lunch or a snack.

But if we're in a meeting, or taking care of children, then we have to focus on our responsibilities. This might make us feel irritable, and so we suppress our irritation to avoid creating additional problems. Being hungry is one problem, being irritable is another, and if we lash out at the children or our colleagues, we've created an additional problem.

The conscious mind generates thoughts which then generate emotions. If we think it's unfair that we have to be in the meeting, then this thought generates negative emotions.

As our mind wanders, we might regret taking this job and wish we'd pursued another line of work. We may feel frustrated that our parents didn't do more to help us, or we might feel anxious about finances.

Alternatively, we might give ourselves credit for sticking with this job, and appreciate what we've learned.

Our conscious minds are always observing and thinking, and these observations and thoughts generate emotions which the conscious mind manages by suppressing them or by fueling them.

It's not natural for us to stand aside from our own thoughts and emotions and observe this flow objectively. This skill of detached observation of our own thoughts and emotions must be learned.

The third layer of complexity is our social life.

Our Social Complexities

Humans are both individuals and social animals. We have to manage ourselves and our complicated relationships with others. Our own needs and wishes are mixed in with the needs and wants of our family, friends, neighbors, co-workers, employer, etc.

This mix generates conflicts that have to be negotiated. In many cases, the easiest way to resolve the conflict is to suppress our own wishes.

Our social life depends on this suppression. When another driver cuts us off, we avoid conflict because this would disrupt not only our life but the flow of traffic. We suppress our annoyance for our own good and for the good of others.

Though we share the same legal rights, we are not all equal in ability and talent. These differences generate conflicting emotions which must be managed.

Some individuals have a natural knack for languages, art, math, music or sports. Those of us without these abilities must work hard just to become mediocre. Those blessed with superior talents might have difficulty understanding why the rest of us struggle.

Other individuals have difficulty empathizing with others, while other individuals have a natural empathy. Aptitudes are not just cognitive; they are also creative and emotional.

Social status is also not equal. For example, our place in the family plays a role in our development. The eldest child has a different experience than the middle child, as does the only child. In some families, the eldest is favored, in others, far more is demanded of the eldest.

There are many sources of inequality in our upbringing. Our parents may have had few ambitions for us and so they didn't nurture our talents. We may feel short-changed when we compare our struggles to the easier path of those whose parents helped them.

Or we might feel suffocated by parents whose ambitions for us which don't align with our own interests or talents. We may resent their ambitions for us because we realize they want us to succeed not for our own happiness but to reflect positively on them.

We might feel obligated to take care of someone and resent the sacrifices we're making. This resentment might make us feel guilty, which makes us feel even worse. We might feel our efforts go unrewarded while others who don't work as hard get unfairly rewarded. There are many potential social-related sources of stress, and these sources are often obscure and complex.

Loss of Meaning

As we go through life, things that worked in one stage might not work in a later stage. Exactly what changed is not always clear to us.

Another complex source of burnout is not recognized by healthcare or economics so it literally does not exist in these fields. Individuals can experience a *crisis of belief or meaning* in which everything they believed and that they thought was meaningful turns to dust.

For example, many of us are trained to think that becoming financially successful is the key to happiness. This is a belief, not a fact. Careful study has found that the quality of our closest relationships is the key to happiness. Over the decades of our lives, having close friends and family is more important to our happiness than financial success.

We sacrifice ourselves for financial success and once we achieve it, we may discover that it's not what we expected. We may find success is more a burden than a source of joy. The beliefs that guided us turn to dust and instead of being happy we feel empty.

This loss of meaning is neither an illness nor a symptom, so the *standards of care* that guide healthcare have no response other than to try to distill this crisis down to a symptom that can be treated by a pill: does this make you anxious? Then here is a pill to reduce your anxiety.

While individual therapists may be sympathetic to a crisis of belief or meaning, the institution of healthcare follows diagnostic and treatment guidelines—*standards of care*--that have no place for an experience which is neither an illness nor a symptom.

For example, the psychiatrist who prescribed my spouse an antidepressant for her burnout depression did not ask her a single question about the circumstances of her burnout. He referred her elsewhere if she wanted "talk therapy."

The socio-economic system also has no means to understand a crisis of belief or meaning. The system reduces all human life to self-interest: humans seek to maximize their private gains.

The idea that an individual would find maximizing financial gain meaningless does not compute in economics, which only recognizes one reason to earn less money: to increase leisure. There is no place for the idea that people might reject the entire system as counter to their interests.

In other words, the system has no capacity to recognize, much less respond to, a crisis of belief or meaning. Individuals who are experiencing a loss of meaning must turn to sources of insight outside healthcare and economics.

For many of us, burnout is the process of peeling the onion of what we thought was meaningful until we find there's nothing left. Burnout strips us of the ability to continue sacrificing ourselves for something which has been revealed as empty.

This crisis can also arise from many sources. Perhaps we tried to work in a conventional setting but could never fit in. Perhaps we tried so hard to meet others' needs that we lost ourselves.

Crises of belief or meaning can also arise from a collapse of our identity. We've told ourselves that our lifestyle of overwork and stress is fulfilling, that it has meaning, that this is who we are.

Then burnout causes us to question these assumptions. Maybe we actually don't like the way we're living; maybe it's no longer fulfilling, and we realize this is not who we really are.

In a crisis of belief or meaning, we may feel confused and lost: why is this happening to me? We may feel that nobody understands us. We may feel tremendous pressure to resume the life we no longer believe in. Friends might ask, "what happened to you?" and we don't have an answer because we don't yet understand what happened to us. We only know that our sense of what is meaningful has changed.

Viewing this as an illness to be cured is the wrong analogy, akin to calling the human mind a computer. Trying to fit a loss of meaning into an economic box is also the wrong analogy: we've entered territories our society and economy don't even recognize.

This is why virtually everything I read about burnout when I was trying to understand what I was experiencing rang false. None of it spoke to what I was experiencing, which was something that could not be cured by a week off or by getting a new job.

None of it helped me understand what I was experiencing. It was all aimed at returning the burnout to the life that had burned us out.

Work that had once been meaningful and fulfilling was no longer so.

The conventional view insists that this crisis is just another label for stress and exhaustion which can be treated with conventional therapies and prescriptions.

But a loss of meaning is not just a fancy sounding synonym for psychological disorders or exhaustion. It is a third kind of experience that cannot be reduced to symptoms or disorders.

The conventional view is that burnout is caused by overwork and stress, and so the cure for burnout is to reduce one's workload.

In my experience, this picture is incomplete.

If we think back over our lives, we can recall times when we were busy and productive, but we didn't feel overworked, stressed or depressed. We slept well and were energized. When we're burning out, the same workload is crushing, our stress levels are high, we sleep poorly and feel drained and depressed.

Is it really the workload that's the source of burnout, or is it that we're no longer getting any reward from our work? By reward I mean a sense of accomplishment, purpose, meaning, a feeling that we're fulfilling our authentic selves, making progress on our life goals and enjoying life.

In my experience, overwork and stress are symptoms, not causes. They are manifestations of a simple truth: something is broken in our life.

Discovering what is no longer working is difficult, because many of the dynamics of human life operate beneath our conscious awareness. As outlined above, our healthcare system is set up to treat illnesses and symptoms. If therapy is part of the *standard of care*, it is brief, as *time is money*. If you need more than a few sessions of therapy, you will likely be paying for much or even all of the costs.

Summary of Complex Sources of Burnout

Let's summarize what I found useful to my understanding of burnout.

To free ourselves of burnout, we must identify the sources of our burnout. If we only treat symptoms, we'll continue to be burned out.

In my experience, there are numerous potential sources of stress within every individual and our socio-economic system.

Given the structure of the human mind and our complex social nature, we're bound to experience conflicting goals, priorities, obligations, loyalties, etc., in ourselves and in our relations with others.

Another source is our maladaptive attempts to overcome the insecurities of growing up in a family that did not validate or nurture us. These maladaptive attempts—for example, projecting an *ideal self* to win others' approval--don't actually make us more secure; they add another layer of stress which can accelerate our descent into burnout.

The nature of work has changed, and so have the financial system, economy and society. Many of these changes increase pressure on workers while reducing the rewards of their work.

Even if we navigate all these pressures and succeed in gaining high status and pay, we may experience a crisis of belief and meaning that spirals into burnout.

To reach renewal, we must first get through the reckoning—identifying the sources of our burnout and eliminating or reducing them.

In my experience, two questions illuminate our search for our burnout's causes:

Why have the *rewards* of our work declined while the *sacrifices* draining us have soared?

What do we rely on to make us feel good about ourselves and our life?

Chapter Five: How Do We Feel Good About Ourselves?

In my experience, we shape our lives to increase whatever makes us feel good about ourselves. We're motivated to do more of whatever gets us noticed and praised.

Our identity—how we think of ourselves—is tied to what makes us feel good about ourselves. For example, being hard working makes us feel good about ourselves and so it becomes part of our identity. Our self-respect is validated by the admiration we get by working hard.

When burnout takes away our ability to work hard, we lose what made us feel good about ourselves.

What makes us feel good about ourselves is not always visible. The process is on automatic pilot: if we found something about ourselves that attracted attention and praise, we felt better about ourselves. Every human wants to be valued and so we latch onto whatever gets us favorably noticed.

If we're attractive, then we use that to gain attention. If we're athletic, we pursue sports. If we're intellectually gifted, we pursue academics. If we're charming, we turn on the charm. If we get praised for helping others, we become helpers. If we have a comic talent, we become the class clown. If leadership comes easily to us, we become leaders. If our talent is artistic, we pursue music or the arts.

If we have money, we buy things that garner attention: lavish homes, luxury cars, art, boats, a particular breed of dog, etc.

Whatever we have that attracts attention and praise *empowers us*. If we lose our looks, talent, house, etc. we feel powerless. Our positive attributes are our source of self-worth. With our positive attributes, we gain more control over our lives—what sociologists call *agency*.

Not everyone is naturally gifted. Most of us are somewhere in the middle. We will probably have to work very diligently to get good enough at something to raise our visibility.

This is one reason why the ability to work hard is so prevalent: it's the most accessible pathway to visibility and praise many of us have.

I was invisible in all my schools, of which there were many as my family moved often. A scrawny, average boy, I was in the basement of athletic talent, good looks, charm and brilliance. As an undersized, shy new kid with no friends, I was the ideal target for bullies.

Undersized and untalented, I was always among the last boys picked for any squad in Physical Education (PE); I was a liability, not an asset. As a new kid in town in the 8th grade, I seemed to be less mediocre in basketball than other sports. Since the school was small, just about anyone could play a sport, I joined the basketball team.

No matter how hard I worked, I would never be as good as players with natural ability improved by experience. But over time I did get better than average kids. I also joined the football team in 10th grade (as a benchwarmer) and tried out for track.

Eventually I was among the first boys picked in PE sports, not because I was talented enough to be first string on any team but because I'd raised myself from the basement to the first floor. My natural talent was still mediocre but I'd raised it to the highest level of my ability.

Being invisible with nothing to feel good about yourself is no fun. Humans are social animals and our prospects in life depend on where we are in the pecking order of visibility and influence.

No wonder we want to become rich and famous; it's how we're wired.

We pursue what empowers us and advances us in the pecking order, which is set by *power relations and constraints*. All social animals are in a sliding scale from powerful to powerless. Being powerless is stressful because you're always vulnerable to the powerful, and it's a disadvantage in terms of attracting mates and opportunities.

There are many kinds of constraints: our height, personality traits, talents, experience, social status, etc.

No human is all-powerful. Every individual has weaknesses and constraints. Even if we escape one constraint, another takes its place.

Even those with the most power struggle to maintain their status.

We're so accustomed to focusing on empowering ourselves that we may not notice that what makes us feel good comes from outside ourselves. None of this recognition and empowerment comes from within ourselves, it all depends on other people.

If we base our identity on being a hard worker, what happens when we burn out and can no longer work at all? Our identity and self-worth crash because they were dependent on the recognition of others.

Losing what we've relied on to make us feel good about ourselves can spiral into depression, deepening our misery and making it harder to climb out of burnout.

If we develop our own inner sources of self-worth, then losing the approval of others due to burnout isn't as devastating: we still have our own sources of identity and self-worth.

How do we develop self-worth that doesn't depend on the approval of others? We base our self-worth on traits that we validate ourselves.

For example, if we feel good about ourselves because we face our problems directly and deal with them upfront, then burning out shifts from being a catastrophic loss of what we relied on to feel good about ourselves to a problem that we face directly and deal with upfront.

Rather than be depressed by the loss of others' approval, we provide our own approval, an approval no one can take away. We give the approval we once received from others to ourselves, even when we're burned out.

We all have the potential to develop the inner resources to face burnout directly and emerge as a more self-reliant person.

Assessing how much of what we relied on to feel good about ourselves came from others is part of burnout's reckoning. The development of inner sources of feeling good about ourselves is part of the renewal.

Gardeners know that plants that are constantly watered never develop deep roots because shallow roots are all that's needed due to the constant watering.

Getting our self-worth from the recognition of others is like getting watered constantly—our self- worth remains shallow. When the flow of approval dries up in burnout, we shrivel up because we don't have deep roots that draw our identity and self-worth from within ourselves.

All humans need something that makes us feel good about ourselves. We can't let go of whatever we rely on now until we've developed an alternative source of feeling good about ourselves.

Once we develop these inner resources, we are liberated from the need to gain the approval of others. We emerge stronger from burnout, far more self-reliant and empowered than we were before.

It's easy to confuse self-reliance and self-sufficiency. Here's one description of the difference: "Self-reliance is control over decision making, whereas self-sufficiency is the fulfillment of physical needs."

In my view, self-reliance is being able to take care of oneself in a variety of circumstances. Skills and experience are integral to self-reliance, but so are trusting our own assessments and judgment, and being flexible and adaptable.

If we draw our sense of self from traits that we validate ourselves, we're free of the shackles of others' approval. This prepares us to be more flexible and open to learning, collaborating and experimenting-- the key dynamics of adapting to new circumstances.

Chapter Six: How Did Work Become the Primary Source of Self-Worth?

Many of us rely on our work to feel good about ourselves. Work provides much of our identity and self-worth. When we can no longer work due to burnout, we lose our source of self-respect. No wonder burnout so often leads to depression. There is very little to feel good about if we relied on work to make us feel good about ourselves.

How did work become the central source of our self-worth?

The easy answer is that work is how we earn money and status, and these define our place in the world. But this answer is incomplete, for there are many non-work-related sources of identity and self-worth.

For example, we can get self-respect from being devoted parents, volunteering in community groups, participating in sports leagues, completing creative projects and sharing the bounty of a productive garden. We can draw our self-worth from facing our problems directly and from being a good friend to ourselves and others. Our personal integrity can be the primary source of our identity.

None of these require a job. So why is work the primary source of self-worth for so many of us?

One is the complex transition of our economy from stability and security to instability and insecurity. This has many sources. (I'll cover two below: *hyper-globalization* and *hyper-financialization*.) The net result is that we're all on our own, and so we have to devote ourselves to work to achieve some security. Korean-German philosopher Byung-Chul Han calls this the *achievement society*. Nobody needs to command us to achieve more, we are our own slave-driving boss.

In his 2010 book *The Burnout Society*, Han says overachievement and overcommunication lead to exhaustion, fatigue and suffocation. He writes, "The *achievement society* is the society of self-exploitation." In other words, we willingly exploit ourselves, constantly seeking to produce more as the price of getting ahead.

In Han's view, we think we're free because we're not beholden to an outside authority: nobody is telling us we have to pursue this career. But this freedom of choice is illusory, as we're imprisoned by our need to achieve, whatever the cost.

We end up working harder than if work were compulsory. Han writes, "This is what makes self-exploitation so efficient." The achiever is both "perpetrator and victim."

In other words, this isn't just healthy ambition to achieve: it's *hyper-achievement*. When *hyper-achievement* becomes our principal goal, we fall into *hyper-self-exploitation* which becomes destructive: we sacrifice everything to achievement. Burnout is our involuntary withdrawal from self-exploitation.

No wonder we've come to depend on our work to make us feel good about ourselves—work is now so all-consuming there isn't much time or energy left for anything else.

Why does this all-consuming work life leave us so prone to burnout?

In Han's analysis, our economic system is not concerned about a *good life*. Its focus is "more capital (income, wealth) produces more life." The more money you make and own, the more expansive your life. But is this life of ever-expanding money and achievement a *good life*? It is certainly profitable for those reaping the gains of the self-exploiting workers, but is it a good life for the self-exploited?

What is a good life? A good life is a life of *self-generated security and well-being*, a balanced life with many sources of fulfillment that aren't dependent on wealth or the approval of others. A good life is a life in which we control the sources of our income, security and self-worth.

The illusion that more achievement and money will lead to a *good life* collapse in burnout. We can no longer exploit ourselves once we burn out.

We accept the notion that more money, status and achievement will deliver the good life, but this dependence on appearances does not create a good life.

Focusing on externalities—our status, what we own, what exotic locale we can brag that we visited—is an exercise in emptiness because none of these generate true security.

In exploiting ourselves for the appearance of success, we get the opposite of what we expected: instead of security and happiness, we get a *crisis of belief and meaning*. We realize these superficialities are fragile and dependent on forces beyond our control: we might lose our job or find our wealth diminished when speculative bubbles pop.

If we've bet our lives on things that are beyond our control, this insecurity is the opposite of the good life: instead of feeling secure, we're anxious about losing things that depend entirely on others.

We burn ourselves out trying to secure more recognition and wealth, thinking that this would make us happy, and then we discover our dependence on work has hollowed us out.

Once money and status are all that we're measuring, it's never enough. If our goal was to be worth $1 million, when we reach that goal, we worry that we might need $2 million. Our goal moves up to $2 million.

We're not striving for a *good life*; we're striving for more of what fuels our insecurity and burnout.

Hyper-Globalization

Another reason we drive ourselves so relentlessly is we are expendable: somebody else can do our job.

Hyper-globalization forced workers in developed countries to compete with a billion poor people in developing nations who had new opportunities for paid work. Since these workers were willing to work for a fraction of the wages paid to developed-nation workers, wages fell around the world when measured by how many work-hours it takes to pay for housing, healthcare, etc.

Economist Michael Spence explained the difference between *tradable work* and *untradable work*. Tradable work can be done anywhere by any group of workers. Untradable work can only be done locally. You can't get a haircut or get your deck repaired overseas.

This interchangeability of parts, software, workers and work is called *commodification*: when something is commodified, it becomes interchangeable with products and services from all over the world. It doesn't matter where the computer chip was fabricated or the bushel of wheat was grown, each chip and bushel serve the same function in the global economy.

Tradable work has also been commodified. It doesn't matter where tech support is located or where software is coded, it's interchangeable with software coded elsewhere. Manufacturing and service industries have been *offshored*, i.e., transferred to countries with lower costs of production due to low wages, lax environmental standards and low-value currencies.

This is Hyper-globalization/financialization = hyper changes in work.

Hyper-Financialization

Untradable work cannot be offshored. But even untradable work has become insecure due to the other major change in our economy, *hyper-financialization*.

Financialization is a complex dynamic, but it basically means two things: 1) financial instruments such as stocks, options, bonds and loans have been commodified and globalized, and 2) borrowing huge sums of money to leverage these instruments makes far more money than producing goods and services, the traditional source of wealth.

In a globalized economy, nobody becomes rich by building a new steel mill in the U.S. They get rich building a steel plant in a low-wage nation and closing the steel mill in the U.S.

In a financialized economy, nobody becomes a billionaire moving the steel mill to a developing nation. They become billionaires by making enormous financial plays that have nothing to do with creating products or jobs. They are purely speculative finance.

The more that the financier can borrow, the bigger the gains. The more money the financier can leverage, the more spectacular the gains.

The key to making money with borrowed money (i.e., financialization) is to 1) leverage $1 billion into a $10 billion bet and 2) reduce risk via financial magic: hedging futures, selling complex derivatives, etc.

Hyper-financialization is when this system of debt and financial magic dominates the real-world economy of producing goods and services.

Those who can tap into this system no longer make millions, they make billions. The wealth of the top few is no longer measured in billions, it's measured in trillions of dollars. This is not just wealth, it is *hyper-wealth*, a world in which $100 million yachts, estates, paintings and private jets are now unremarkable.

The statistics are startling. The top three billionaires in the U.S. own more financial wealth than the bottom half of American households (165 million people in 62 million households). The total wealth of the 614 U.S. billionaires grew from $240 billion in 1990 (adjusted for inflation) to $4.18 trillion in March 2021—a 17-fold increase, while the median wealth of American families barely budged, moving from around $80,000 in 1990 to about $110,000—a trivial gain compared to the enormous gains of the super-wealthy.

In a hyper-financialized economy, those who can borrow and leverage the most make the most money. Since all this wealth is generated by assets such as real estate and stocks, those who bought these assets before they were hyper-financialized have become wealthy by virtue of buying early.

Since the bottom 99.5% can't leverage millions into billions, there's no way we can get hyper-wealthy. Those who bought assets decades ago are now wealthy because the house they bought for $100,000 is now worth $1 million, not because it's ten times bigger or better but because our economy has been hyper-financialized.

This is why the top 10% of American households own 90% of the nation's financial wealth and over 70% of all wealth.

The bottom 50% own a meager 2% of all wealth, which includes vehicles, household items, family homes, etc.

In other words, hyper-globalization and hyper-financialization generate *hyper-inequality*. These forces have changed our economy into a *winner take most* rat-race: a relative few get spectacular paychecks and a few speculators win big, But the vast majority of workers don't earn enough to bridge the wealth gap.

The gap between those who bought homes and stocks decades ago and those trying to buy these assets now is unbridgeable except for those who inherit money or the few speculators who strike it rich and don't lose it all when their luck sours.

A relative few do well in small business, but the financial pressures on small business have increased. It's hard to make a middle-class income after paying all the expenses and taxes, and most proprietors and free-lancers work more hours than employees.

The net income earned by proprietors and free-lancers is also *winner take most*, as the majority of small business income goes to the few at the top.

Faced with this uphill battle to earn enough to buy a house, many people give up on the conventional job market. They work in the informal (cash) economy or in the gig economy, perhaps relying on government subsidies for some expenses. A relative few do well but financial insecurity is never far from the door of most gig workers.

The pressures to exploit oneself are intense in a *winner take most*, highly unequal economy. No wonder work absorbs so much of our time and energy, and why we come to rely on it so much for our self-worth.

This dependence on our job for our self-worth and identity works as long as we can keep up the grueling pace of achievement and self-exploitation. But once burnout strips away our ability to keep up the pace, the downside of this dependence becomes clear: it's not just our work-life that unravels in burnout; our identity and self-worth also collapse.

Chapter Seven: Running on Empty

The title of Jackson Browne's song *Running on Empty* is an apt description of burnout: we're running flat-out to keep everything glued together but our "fuel tank" is on empty.

We're making greater sacrifices while everything we once felt was rewarding rings hollow: *we're too tired to care*. We're not doing all this work because *we want to*—because the rewards of pay and positive feelings about ourselves are so great—we're doing it because *we have to*. If we slow down or cut back, the whole thing falls apart.

Before burnout, the rewards were our focus. As our tanks run dry, we start focusing on the sacrifices, which have increased incrementally even as the rewards have eroded.

As we keep running on empty, our ability to feel anything other than exhaustion declines: we're zombies going through the motions not because the rewards empower us but because we have to make money and keep everything together regardless of the cost to ourselves.

But once our tank is dry, we can only keep *running on empty* for so long before the automatic self-preservation of burnout shuts us down.

The sacrifices required of us have ratcheted higher so incrementally that we haven't noticed that the ratchet only clicks higher, it never drops back to lower levels. We tell ourselves it will get better but it doesn't; the workload and stress only increase.

The rewards appear to be unchanged: we're still getting paid. But the rewards no longer matter. We feel like we're on a treadmill rather than getting ahead. We tell ourselves we're doing what we want but that rings false: the truth is we're too tired to care. Our ability to feel anything other than exhaustion and stress has cliff-dived.

Sacrifice and rewards are a tradeoff that change over time.

When we were vibrant and enthused the sacrifices didn't even feel like sacrifices; they were just the normal grind. The rewards made us feel like we were on the right path.

Once we're running on empty, we no longer think about the future, we only focus on getting through today. Any thoughts of the future tend to be fantasies of running away from our burdens.

Chronic stress undermines our ability to work and diminishes the rewards. As the burdens get heavier, we realize the rewards are not worth the tremendous effort we're making. As we start burning out, we realize our work is suffering, we're becoming forgetful, every day is a slog through a swamp of stress, we no longer enjoy the things we once enjoyed, everything takes extraordinary effort, and as a result our sense that we're going in the right direction has crumbled.

The conventional view on burnout is that all this the result of overwork, and once the burnout dials back their workload and devotes a few precious hours to their own interests, the sacrifices and rewards will be restored to a positive balance.

While this may be true for some burnouts, this superficial "it's just overwork" ignores the sources of chronic stress that are not directly related to being overworked.

The superficial explanation ignores how the nature of work has changed: work is increasingly open-ended. The employee is expected to respond to work demands regardless of other commitments. The self-exploitation of the Achievement Society is also open-ended: there's always another credential to get or another market to tap. The expectations are also open-ended: others are holding up despite the superhuman stress, so you should, too.

The extreme disparities of wealth and power leave many people as second-class citizens, a situation that greatly increases chronic stress. Low income is also a source of chronic stress, as a single misfortune can trigger a domino-like cascade of financial crises without the kind of resolutions available to higher income households.

Many jobs lack *agency*—the amount of power the employees have over their work. This lack of control over our work generates chronic stress.

It's useful to look at the *power relations and constraints* of our circumstances.

The power to make changes can be understood as control, freedom and autonomy. What do we have the power to change without someone else's approval? If we have little leeway to change things and a multitude of constraints, our ability to solve problems is limited.

Whatever we have to make us feel good about ourselves is also power. If that power diminishes, we have less to feel good about ourselves.

As mentioned earlier, the workload we managed easily in the past might now feel impossible, and the rewards that seemed ample back then now feel like crumbs. What changed?

Many things might have changed. As we got older, life got more complicated and our goals and values might have changed without us being fully aware of it.

When we were younger, we felt empowered: if we didn't like a job, we'd look for another one, maybe in a different field. The downside of seeking a job in a new field was modest, as we could always go back to the previous one. If we were tired of a place, we could move; we had few possessions or obligations. There were fewer constraints on us: we only had ourselves to worry about and our needs were few.

Now that we're older, it's difficult to change anything without disrupting our entire life. We can't find work in a new field because the pay will be low for new entrants. We can't move because we'd have to sell our house. The decision isn't ours alone anymore; our spouse loves their job and family and friends bind us to this place.

For all the reasons described above, we have less power over our work than before, and the sacrifices necessary to keep whatever power we have increased as *hyper-achievement* demands ever greater sacrifices just to keep from falling behind. Employees are told they have flexibility but this boils down to working harder and longer. If we're self-employed, the burdens of operating costs keep increasing.

Feeling powerless and strapped down is unsettling. We go over the same ground, seeking a solution which doesn't exist. We try to regain some control on the margins of our life, but these adjustments are too small to make a difference: we're still running on empty.

As what little left in the tank is devoted to work, there's less left for our family, friends and recreation. Our joy in life has faded; we go through the motions but no longer feel much of anything. Socializing feels more like a burden than a joy. We're too exhausted to cook so we eat junk food and are too tired to stay fit, so our health declines.

The things in our lives that once offset the burdens of work go by the wayside, as we no longer have the energy to keep them going: work takes all that we have in the tank.

Those around us try to understand but end up annoyed by our constant exhaustion. They're frustrated that we no longer care about anything but getting through the day. The only person who can really understand us is another burnout, and if we don't know anyone who burned out and recovered, we end up feeling alone and isolated. It's easy to slip into self-pity: nobody understands me.

Beset by stress and isolation, we may seek to self-medicate, and this adds another layer of problems to our lives. We may become dependent on alcohol, drugs or medications to get through the day. But since self-medication doesn't address the source of our stress, its negative consequences only increase our burdens.

By this stage we're in danger of damaging our health.

When the last drop is drained from the tank, there's nothing left to keep us going, and we burn out.

Chapter Eight: What Changed?

Those who have known us a long time may be mystified by our burnout because they don't see any changes that seem big enough to trigger such a life-changing collapse. They may not have seen the stress ratcheting higher, or the increasing constraints and powerlessness.

They can't see what's changed inside us, and we may not be able to tell them because we're only dimly aware of these changes ourselves.

The general expectation is for everyone to be cheerful and positive because we always have choices: if life gives you lemons, make lemonade. If you don't like your job, get another one. If you don't like your house, move.

Yes, everyone has choices. But these choices are constrained by our agency (i.e., control of our lives), wealth, character, locale, education, etc., and who's permission we need to make major changes.

Once we burn out, we no longer have the energy to make big changes like moving to a new locale or changing careers. We can't face these tasks until we've recovered.

The previous chapters covered the incremental increases in stress that over time can add up to crushing burdens. This chapter looks at the changes within us that transform our perception of the sacrifices we're making and the rewards we're getting.

When what we rely on to feel good about ourselves is no longer working, we question what's meaningful. Maybe our circumstances haven't changed; maybe *we've changed*.

These changes don't announce themselves. We don't wake up one morning and say, "I've changed." These changes occur beneath the surface of our busy lives. It's like the season changed but we didn't notice it as we were occupied by our daily lives.

Another reason we aren't aware of how much our feelings have changed is we are deeply committed to whatever we've invested so much of ourselves to build—a career, home, family and financial stake.

Our first impulse is to protect this investment from anything that threatens to upset it, including our own feelings.

We tell ourselves we like our job, home and prospects as a way of talking ourselves out of any doubts we might have. But telling ourselves what we should feel doesn't change what we really feel. We can suppress the feeling that something is broken but we can't reverse it.

We fear changes in ourselves because the consequences are unpredictable: if we admit our feelings have changed, won't this upend our life? Rather than face these uncertainties, we try to persuade ourselves into agreeing that these feelings are just a temporary slump.

But whatever isn't working keeps gnawing away at us until we finally break.

Since these changes occur beneath the surface of our conscious awareness, they may manifest as changes in behavior rather than as flashes of insight. Since we repress our feelings, they may come to the surface as actions.

Rather than admit to ourselves that our marriage is no longer working, we have an affair. Rather than admit to ourselves we hate our job, we get fired. If we're self-employed, we torpedo an expansion that would have required more work, or cling to a business our burnt-out partner desperately wants to sell.

Our conscious minds are adept at inventing cover stories for our sabotage: my boss was a jerk, etc.

Though we do our best to hide our feelings, we can't hide them all the time, not even from ourselves. We become frustrated with ordinary problems, and find ourselves fantasizing about running away to a new life. As the pressure builds within us, our health suffers. We may develop chronic illnesses or have a medical emergency.

What changed without us being fully aware of it? Maybe we're tired of our work-life and finally had enough. Maybe we're under more pressure even as our income is increasingly insecure. Perhaps we've gone as far as we can go and we no longer want to spend the rest of our life spinning the same wheels.

We can also tire of a locale. Maybe we've wrung every drop of value out of it and there's nothing left to keep us here except habit. Maybe our neighborhood has decayed. Maybe the commute has finally worn us down. Maybe we don't want to live like this anymore.

As painful as it may be, we can tire of a relationship. Maybe we're tired of our spouse or partner having most of the power and resisting our efforts to balance it more fairly. Maybe we're tired of supporting difficult family members. Perhaps we're tired of having to negotiate everything as a constant power struggle. Perhaps we feel our spouse doesn't make an effort to understand us or support us. Maybe we're both burned out.

Seasons of Life

We also change as we age. My experience of burnout at 65 was different from my burnout at 33. When I burned out at 33, I no longer had the mental or emotional capacity to work so many hours under such unrelenting pressure, but my physical strength remained intact. What drove me to despair was my sense of failure.

At 65, not only could I no longer work so many hours under never-ending stress, I was physically exhausted, too; it now took extraordinary effort to do the smallest tasks. At 33, I was a hollowed-out zombie; at 65, I was completely intolerant of any source of stress.

As we age, our expectations and perceptions change. What worked in our 20s no longer works in our 30s, what worked in our 30s no longer works in our 40s, what worked in our 40s no longer works in our 50s, what worked in our 50s no longer works in our 60s and what worked in our 60s no longer works in our 70s.

In my experience, there are key inflection points in our lives, periods where dramatic changes tend to occur. One such period is our late teens and early 20s when we choose careers, educational pathways and spouses. We are eager for experience and may move, travel, or change jobs. We may embrace entrepreneurship and launch a new business or join a fledgling enterprise. We embrace change and risk.

A second period in which life changes are common is our mid to late 30s: if we're going to make the move to an entirely different career, this often happens in this time frame. Relationships formed in our late teens and 20s may break apart in this period, businesses are closed and major moves to a new locale occur. We either reconcile ourselves to the loss of a dream or we decide to pursue it before it's too late.

We take stock of where the choices we made in our 20s have taken us, and if we feel stymied, we realize it's a *now or never* moment to change course, as the energy needed to make a big change may diminish and the window of opportunity may close.

We ask ourselves: is this all I'll ever have? If the answer is unsatisfactory, then we take the risk of making big changes, knowing it may be our last chance to pursue whatever we set aside along the way.

The period of our late 50s to mid-60s is another period of appraisal and decision. As we age, our energy flags and working hard now takes a toll. We may feel we've done all we can in our work-life and want to pursue interests that aren't so focused on making money. We may be ready to fulfill dreams of travel or new pursuits.

Or we may be forced to reshuffle our lives to care for elderly parents or grandchildren, or both. We take stock of what we have and accept that it's likely to be all we'll have unless we make a major change now.

We may realize that something we gave up as impractical or too risky in our late 30s is still a possibility, but only if we act decisively now while we still have sufficient energy and will to make it happen.

Burnout can occur at any point in adulthood, but in my case, it occurred in these windows of major change, the 30s and the 60s, when whatever worked in the previous decade no longer works, and whatever we kept glued together finally breaks us. We will ourselves to go on but we can't; whatever once refilled our tank has been lost.

The disconnect between what we feel—exhausted, at a dead end--and what we have to do to keep it all glued together widens. The more we have to do, the less we feel like doing it. The sources of stress never diminish, they only increase.

If the sacrifices required of us far outweigh the rewards, we may have made what I call a *Devil's Pact* without being aware of it.

Devil's Pacts

In the classic *Devil's Pact*, an individual willingly signs away their eternal soul to the Devil in return for a power that is otherwise out of reach— immortality here on Earth, great wealth, etc. It is only when the Devil comes to claim his prize that the individual realizes that what they traded away is far more valuable than what they received in return.

In the context of burnout, the Devil's Pact is with ourself. We convince ourselves to accept compromises that are bad deals for us. As the deals become progressively worse, we burn out.

We trade away our *agency*—control of our lives--in exchange for a *half-measure* that gives us some security but at a cost that's far higher than we realize. Over time, the sacrifices increase while the benefits diminish, and we burn out.

Burnout gives us an opportunity to understand that what we traded away was so much more valuable than what we received, but in our insecurity, we took the deal as the best available. Fearful of losing what we have, we cling to the Devil's Pact until we burn out.

What do we get in a Devil's Pact? We get a focus and purpose. We accept a half-measure that serves others' interests so we don't have to take the risks of finding a purpose that serves our best interests.

We get a half-measure of security and self-worth, but these are always contingent on others' approval and control. As the demands for further sacrifice increase, we cling on to the source of our purpose, security and self-worth until burnout takes it away.

We need to differentiate *tradeoffs* from *Devil's Pacts*, as they appear similar. Let's say I'm offered two jobs. Each has advantages.

The first job has a much longer commute than my previous job but I like the managers, my co-workers and the working environment. The values guiding the workplace align with my own: clear communication, open management style, etc., and I'd get a modest raise.

The longer commute is the tradeoff I have to accept to take the job.

The second job's advantage is a big pay raise and financial security a step above my current job. But the management seems adept at saying one thing but doing another, and the work environment is tense. The customer service is poor and support of overworked employees thin. I'd have to let go of my standards and accept dictatorial, erratic managers. My control of my work would be marginal at best.

The first job requires a *tradeoff*: it's a good fit for *who I am* but I'll have to accept the longer commute. Workarounds are available. Maybe I can rideshare and ask my spouse to pick up the kids after school.

The second job is a *Devil's Pact*: it's not a fit for *who I am* and there's no workaround for a toxic workplace. The benefit--the higher pay—is limited but the sacrifices required are open-ended.

If I take the first job, I sacrifice the time required by the commute. This is a constraint and a cost but it's predictable. The commute will vary day to day but the full cost is known.

If I take the Devil's Pact because of the extra money, I'm entering a workplace that violates *who I am*. What I'll have to sacrifice is open-ended. The sacrifices might start small but end up eating me alive.

We don't see it when we accept the deal, but Devil's Pacts are greased slides to burnout because there are no limits on what's demand of us while what we gain will always be limited.

What's missing in this example is a third *whole hog / full measure* option in which I accept the risk of failure in exchange for full control of my work and the gains of my work—an option where I retain control of my life. If I fail, I absorb the losses, but if I succeed, the gains are mine.

In other words, what if I didn't have to accept open-ended sacrifices for limited rewards which I don't control and which could diminish?

In Devil's Pacts, we have little control and so the risk of others' failures fall on us. Meanwhile, our rewards are limited. It's a bad deal for us.

Why do we accept bad deals?

We're fearful. What if we fail? What if we end up alone? The familiar feels safer than the unknown, even when what's familiar is a bad deal for us. We're so afraid of ending up with nothing that we overlook just how bad a deal we're accepting.

Deep down, perhaps we fear we aren't worthy of a deal that works for us. It takes confidence in ourselves to accept the risk that we might fail. But if we can't accept any risk, we lose the chance to be rewarded far beyond what we'll ever get in a Devil's Pact.

We may have accepted a position that wasn't a Devil's Pact at first but it became a Devil's Pact when management or other conditions changed. Do we accept the Devil's Pact because the familiar is safer than the unknown, or do we leave and take our chances?

If we don't need others' approval, we're better prepared to risk a move than those who lack self-confidence and inner sources of self-worth.

Failure is not enjoyable but it's also not the end of the world that so many fear. In my experience, we learn far more from failure than we do from success. As Aeschylus observed, "There is advantage in the wisdom won from pain."

No one can spare us the ups and downs of our voyage through life. As novelist Marcel Proust wrote, "We don't receive wisdom; we must discover it for ourselves after a journey that no one can take for us or spare us."

We accept Devil's Pacts because we think accepting a half-measure is better than risking the unknown. But the essence of a Devil's Pact is the downside is open-ended but the upside is limited.

It's a battle we cannot win because others control the pieces on the board. Sun Tzu wrote, "If a battle cannot be won, do not fight it." Devil's Pacts cannot be won but we accept them rather than choose battles we might win.

Many people stay in Devil's Pacts their entire adult lives. They stay in misery-producing relationships and jobs they don't like until they pass away. They are too fearful to let go of a known bad deal for an unknown deal which could be even worse.

The burnout has the opportunity to see the Devil's Pact for what it truly is, an open-ended sacrifice of self for crumbs of security, a familiarity we chafe under but are too fearful to relinquish.

Lopsided relationships are one type of Devil's Pact. *The martyr* chooses situations where their sacrifice is highlighted for others to admire; *the helper* keeps the troubled person glued together just enough to stay troubled so they can remain the saintly helper; *the stern parent* is bossy for everyone else's own good—whether they consider being controlled and cajoled good or not; *the daredevil* takes inordinate risks to prove their courage and strength; the *drama-trauma addict* chooses situations that are always in turmoil so they can blame their problems on others; *the monk* cuts themselves off from everyone to reduce their suffering; the *go along to get along* passively suffers to avoid triggering conflicts; the *negotiator* contests everything to come out ahead, no matter how trivial; the *critic* builds themselves up by cutting everyone else down; *it's the money, honey* stays in dysfunctional relationships for the financial benefits, and the *too fearful to leave* clings to dysfunctional relationships and jobs they loathe.

In situations where one person feels good about themselves at the expense of others the bully/abuser has truly sold their soul to the Devil.

Another Devil's Pact is to sacrifice everything else in our life to the goal of becoming successful as measured in recognition and wealth. A common midlife crisis occurs when those who sacrificed everything for status and wealth achieve their goal and then discover that their success is hollow: it didn't transform their insecurity into security.

When they discover this isn't how it works—self-worth only comes from within—they may experience a crisis of meaning.

In Devil's Pacts, we don't understand what we're sacrificing; we're only aware that accepting the *Devil's Pact* relieves our anxiety and gives us something to feel good about in the here and now.

The key characteristic of the Devil's Pact is that we don't have an alternative way to feel good about ourselves, so we accept the Devil's Pact because whatever half-measure we get is better than nothing.

If we had a better option, we'd take it, but we don't.

Everyone under the thumb of the *stern parent*, the *negotiator*, the *critic, the bully* or the *drama-trauma addict* wishes to be free of their demands. Everyone listening to *it's the money, honey* or *too fearful to leave* complain about being trapped wishes they'd muster up the courage to leave their dysfunctional relationship or job.

In other words, *Devil's Pacts* are not sources of happiness. They are prisons for everyone who's forced to live with the distortions and miseries. Those in the Pact fear losing their source of security—yes, it's miserable, but it's comfortingly familiar--no matter how destructive it is because they have no other source of feeling good about themselves.

If we abandon the Pact, then what will we focus on? Take away the anxiety and stress, and what's left? We can't imagine being happy because that would require abandoning our Devil's Pact and we can't imagine living without the turmoil that gives us focus and purpose.

Feeling trapped in problems that can't be resolved gives us purpose, and so we devote ourselves to keeping our problems unresolvable. Resolving the problem would take away our purpose.

The possibility that our woes may be largely self-inflicted doesn't occur to us. Perhaps we feel that being trapped by problems which can't be resolved is all we deserve. Maybe managing dysfunction is a powerful source of feeling competent and needed.

Having problems that can't be resolved gives us a reason to feel self-empathy: I'm trapped in a job where no one appreciates me and a dysfunctional relationship in which I'm not valued.

We want to think of ourselves as someone who earns admiration by struggling along with unresolvable problems. That we sabotage any way out of these problems doesn't occur to us.

Once we're burned out our problems are no longer unresolvable. One by one our Devil's Pacts unravel and everything crashes.

We thought we were trapped, but burnout removes barriers by taking away our ability to keep the Pacts glued together.

Burnout doesn't resolve our problems but it dismantles our ability to keep them unresolvable. Burnout doesn't eliminate our attraction to Devil's Pacts, but it eliminates our ability to maintain them.

Burnout doesn't respond to whatever we tell ourselves. It is a mechanism of self-preservation that is beyond our conscious control. Burnout is impervious to our conscious demands.

Director Juzo Itami's film *Tampopo*, generally classified as a comedy, includes a brief scene that is darkly surreal. A housewife lays dying in her cramped home. Her husband cajoles her to get up and make dinner for him and the children: we're hungry. Caving in to his incessant demands, she drags herself to the kitchen, makes a simple meal, puts it on the table and then slips into the embrace of death. The husband is too busy slurping up his dinner to notice.

This is a dramatic depiction of Devil's Pacts and burnout. Like the dying housewife, the burnout makes extraordinary efforts to do what others expect of them.

The burnout isn't just exhausted. We're exhausted by the distortions and miseries we've imposed on ourselves and those around us.

Burnout is the death of whatever bad deal gave us focus, purpose and a few shreds of self-worth.

We don't want to hear that what worked for us for so long is broken. We don't want to hear about our insecurities and *Devil's Pacts*. We don't want to hear that we can't make burnout go away, or that it will change our life whether we want these changes or not.

We don't want to hear what burnout is telling us: we exceeded our limit and we can't go on.

Burnout is an opportunity to reorganize our life so we no longer need Devil's Pacts. The individual who draws upon their entire self for their self-worth doesn't need to trade away their life for the comfortingly familiar miseries of Devil's Pacts.

Let's return to this chapter's question: What's changed?

Something much larger scale also changed.

Our Economy's Devil's Pact

Our economy made its own *Devil's Pact*. To understand what has been sacrificed, let's begin with a comment French writer Michel Houellebecq made in an interview: *"I have the impression of being caught up in a network of complicated, minute, stupid rules, and I have the impression of being herded towards a uniform kind of happiness, toward a kind of happiness that doesn't really make me happy."*

The *Achievement Economy* herds us into an open-ended demand for higher productivity with the promise that the rewards of our hard work will make us happy. But this "uniform kind of happiness" serves the desires of others at the cost of ourselves.

Telling ourselves we're happy doesn't mean we're actually happy. Telling others that we're happy doesn't mean we're happy. It just means we want to present ourselves as happy to gain approval.

The Achievement Economy is implicitly based on the ideal of *no limits*: no limits on ambition and achievement, no limits on wealth or the Earth's resources, no limits on what we can accomplish *if only we devote ourselves to it 100%.*

This is the ideal parroted in countless narratives of average people achieving greatness through single-minded devotion to success.

But there are limits: there are physical limits imposed by physics and chemistry, limits on the planet's resources, and limits what we can sacrifice without burning out.

Houellebecq references Alexis De Tocqueville's classic book, *Democracy in America* (1840). Here is an excerpt from Volume II, Chapter Six, that aptly describes the quiet tyranny of the Achievement Economy:

"The will is not shattered, but softened, bent, and guided: men are seldom forced by it to act, but they are constantly restrained from acting: such a power does not destroy... it does not tyrannize, but it compresses, enervates, extinguishes and stupefies a people, till the nation is reduced to being nothing better than a flock of timid and industrious animals."

As noted previously, in the Achievement Economy, we're our own slave-driving boss. Since the demands on us are open-ended, we can never work enough. In some sense we never stop working, and so there is less time for anything else in our life. Our connections to others still exist but they weaken and become superficial. Our social ties and relationships wither as work dominates our life.

We become *atomized*, disconnected, each in our own world.

In discussing the atomization of the individual, Houellebecq quotes this passage from *Democracy in America*:

"Each of them, living apart, is as a stranger to the fate of all the rest-- his children and his private friends constitute to him the whole of mankind; as for the rest of his fellow-citizens, he is close to them, but he sees them not--he touches them, but he feels them not; he exists but in himself and for himself alone."

Houellebecq then adds: *"This passage contains almost all of my written work. I just had to add one thing, and that is that the person who still has friends and family in Tocqueville no longer has them with me. The disconnection process is complete."*

We rebel at this description of our economy as a force that atomizes us into individuals with few meaningful bonds to friends and family and even fewer to fellow-citizens.

We rebel at this dispiriting depiction until we burn out. Then we discover the truth of De Tocqueville's bleak vision: we really are alone. We're expected to get back to being a timid, industrious pack animal.

We told ourselves we were happy, and perhaps we were in the sense that the Devil's Pact worked for us for a time. But something changed. We can no longer act as if there are no limits, for we've reached our own limits: we cannot make our burnout disappear.

Summary of What's Changed

What changed? We hit our limits and burned out.

Where do we start in understanding our burnout? We can start by asking questions which we avoid as difficult and perhaps painful. What are we without work and the *ideal self* we present to others?

Burnout offers us an opportunity to ask another important question: can we imagine being happy? Not the *poor-me payoff* of Devil's Pacts, but real happiness: freedom from the chains and miseries of hyper-achievement and Devil's Pacts, authentic fulfillment from within ourselves rather than saying we're happy as if saying it makes it so.

If we can't even imagine being truly happy with ourselves and our life, then how can we get there? Burnout opens up the potential to reimagine our lives not as a series of Devil's Pacts but as a fulfillment of being ourselves.

Thomas Merton said—and I paraphrase—God wants us to be ourselves; God doesn't want us to try to be someone else. You don't have to believe in God to understand that the idealized self we present to others is trying to be someone else. We're trying to be something we're not because we think that will make us happy, when being ourselves is the only real source of fulfillment.

Chapter Nine: Acquiring Yourself

The purpose of the previous two chapters was to explore this simple statement: *burnout has changed me.* As I said at the end of Chapter Three, *burnout is an involuntary intolerance for what no longer works in our lives.* What no longer works generates chronic stress and so we burn out.

I also said that *burnout is a reckoning and an opportunity for renewal, a gift that can be rejected or accepted.* If we insist that burnout hasn't changed us and we can strap ourselves right back into whatever burned us out, in my view that is rejecting an opportunity for renewal.

In my experience, burnout raises this question: *who am I, really?* If we refuse to ask this question or insist that we haven't changed at all, we've decided to cling to whatever burned us out. Cause and effect: same circumstance, same effect: burnout.

If we accept that if want to emerge from burnout, our circumstances have to change, that raises this question: what changes do we need to make to eliminate the sources of burnout?

The simple answer is "eliminate sources of chronic stress." This is a practical approach. But in my view, *burnout is the result of our circumstances not serving who we really are.* We put our energy into achieving success, and the net result was we burned out.

We told ourselves we were serving our own interests and that we were happy, but burnout shredded those rationalizations. Going back to what caused burnout is not a solution to burnout.

To figure out how best to change our circumstances, we first have to first figure out who we really are and then make a realistic assessment of our circumstances: what are our options, and what constrains them?

Without this self-awareness, we're unlikely to gain a recovery from burnout and a renewal of our enthusiasm for life.

The next two chapters present pathways to self-awareness that I found useful. They may strike some readers as too philosophic to be practical.

In my experience, self-knowledge is inherently elusive, and shortcuts touted as practical tend to be dead-ends.

In other words, I present these two chapters as more practical than shortcuts based on personality tests and checklists—the usual shortcuts in our *achievement society*. But as I said at the start, I am only sharing what helped me. These pathways may not be helpful to you.

With this in mind, let's give it a try anyway, shall we?

You've heard the expression *finding yourself*. This presumes some part of ourselves has been abandoned along the way and is out there somewhere awaiting our rediscovery. To find it, we must search for our lost self. There is some intuitive truth in this, as the trade-offs we've made may have required abandoning some aspects of ourselves.

Danish philosopher Soren Kierkegaard used a different phrase which translates as *acquire yourself*. As my wife and I each struggled to make sense of our burnout, we found ourselves drawn to the works of Thomas Merton and Kierkegaard. (More on Merton in a moment.)

Kierkegaard was a Christian who wrote extensively on faith. But he also addressed the human condition and the choices presented to each of us. He wrote dense, difficult books which I do not claim to understand. As a burnout, I was interested in what he meant by *acquiring oneself* because this struck me as an essential step in the process of understanding my own burnout and clearing a path to renewal.

For Kierkegaard, the process of acquiring oneself is not just rediscovering ourselves but *creating ourselves*. This is the goal and purpose of life. He wrote: *"...if you have, or rather if you will to have the requisite energy, you can win what is the chief thing in life—win yourself, acquire you own self."*

The phrase *finding yourself* implies there is a lost self that awaits discovery, and finding it will restore our authentic self.

Acquiring yourself suggests an active process of discovery and creation. The process isn't limited to searching for what's been lost, it's acquiring yourself through action.

Acquiring yourself is a process of adding a new piece to yourself every day: we don't find an already complete self that was abandoned in the past, we acquire a self by assembling aspects of ourselves, some rediscovered, some new, one action at a time.

We may rediscover forgotten interests and talents which we then develop and express, but the process doesn't require finding a talent that was abandoned. We can start from scratch.

The key to acquiring ourself is that the self we acquire doesn't depend on the recognition or approval of others. For example, if we acquire personal integrity, this is a trait that is within us. We don't acquire integrity by getting someone to praise us. Integrity doesn't depend on how we look or what others think of us or what wealth we pile up.

If we acquire the ability to be completely honest with ourselves, nobody can see this to approve or disapprove. Only we know that we've acquired the ability to be completely honest with ourselves.

Burnout is the result of sacrificing our advancement as an individual for whatever we relied on to feel good about ourselves. Acquiring ourselves is the process of replacing whatever external sources we relied on with internal sources that are not dependent on others.

The core of acquiring ourselves is to advance our *self-knowledge* and *self-expression*. Acquiring oneself includes being true to ourselves, but it also means expressing ourselves through our choices and actions.

In acquiring ourself, we provide our own sources of feeling good about ourselves by advancing our *self-knowledge* and *self-expression*. Self-knowledge is not a place we reach; it is a lifelong learning process.

As we age and our circumstances change, we change and so we are constantly learning more about ourselves and piecing together a better understanding of our experiences, goals and inner life.

Self-expression is also a continual learning process as we seek to express our authentic interests, talents and sources of fulfillment. By authentic I mean sources of fulfillment beyond credentials, wealth, and recognition, all of which are external acquired rather than bestowed by ourselves to ourselves.

 Credentials may be a necessary step to reach a place where we can express ourselves fully. But there is a difference between relying on the credential to feel good about ourselves and feeling good about being able to express ourselves by the practice of the skills we learned.

Bruce Lee was an influential martial artist and film star. He was a student of philosophy and this is reflected in his writings about martial arts. Lee famously said: *"To me, ultimately, martial art means honestly expressing yourself."*

This is remarkably different from the usual descriptions of martial arts as self-defense, physical development or attaining a high level of skill that is reflected in a top ranking—for example, becoming a black belt.

Lee also said: *"Actually I do not, you know, teach karate, because I do not believe in style. If you do not have style, you can just say, here I am, you know, as a human being. How can I express myself, totally and completely?"*

Self-expression can't be copied or borrowed. Lee wrote: *"Always be yourself, express yourself, have faith in yourself, do not go out and look for a successful personality and duplicate it."*

Lee's insights help us understand the difference between an individual who has acquired the ability to honestly express themselves, and an individual who draws their identity and self-worth from externalities such as credentials and the recognition of others.

For this person, earning the black belt is not just a source of pride but the ultimate goal of martial arts: others will respect me, admire me and perhaps fear me.

For Bruce Lee, the value of achieving this accomplishment is to enable one's self-expression: the more you know about something, the wider the possibilities for self-expression. For Lee, the point wasn't to master a martial arts style and be recognized for this mastery; it was to escape the limits of styles entirely by seeking to express oneself.

Kierkegaard saw these choices as either/or: one cannot serve two masters. In Kierkegaard's view, everything important required a full commitment.

My interpretation is that if we spend most of our effort on external sources of identity and self-worth, it isn't possible to acquire self-knowledge and self-expression because these are difficult and require our full commitment. To acquire oneself requires changing our view of what life is about and what is important for our advancement.

When we acquire ourselves, we acquire all of ourselves, not just the parts we're proud of or the parts we like. We are also willing to embrace being impatient, prideful, fearful, anxious, potentially self-destructive, glory-seeking, prone to self-pity, etc. They're part of the package of being human. They are not flaws; they are our teachers.

As you might imagine given his views on 100% commitment, Kierkegaard believed the goal of life was pursuing whatever made us enthusiastic, stimulated, interesting in learning more and doing more.

Kierkegaard saw enthusiasm as equal opportunity: everyone can feel enthusiasm and express themselves. It doesn't matter how much or how little talent we have, we are all equal in our potential to follow our interests with enthusiasm.

If the point is no longer to accomplish something external, then every enthusiasm and interest is an opportunity to express ourselves. The more we learn, the greater our opportunities to find fulfillment in expressing ourselves.

In my view, the power of Kierkegaard's idea of acquiring yourself is it offers a roadmap for giving ourselves a positive identity and source of feeling good about ourselves that we control, that isn't dependent on others or on externalities such as credentials.

What matters isn't our talent or level of accomplishment or our financial success or the recognition we gain. What matters is expressing ourselves as unique individuals.

In my experience, life requires tradeoffs, and there is no perfection in which we make lots of money expressing ourselves. A few people manage to do so, but I certainly don't want to set that unrealistic standard as the measure of my life.

If we can find a livelihood that gives us some small measure of self-expression, that may be the best that can be done. We may have a job that offers us no self-expression. In that case, how we conduct ourselves is our self-expression.

We may find fulfillment in a way of living as well as in pursuing our interests. Thomas Merton found fulfillment as a Trappist monk, one of the Catholic church's religious orders. Merton was a writer at a young age and continued writing after he became a monk.

Self-expression should not be limited by preconceptions. Our enthusiasms may be fulfilled in a brief exploration of a subject, or they may last a lifetime. Our interests may wax and wane. We might drop something and pick it back up years later. Our interests might be valuable to others or they might have no financial value.

What matters is their value to us as sources of enthusiasm and avenues of self-expression. The range of self-expression is as infinite as individuality.

Chapter Ten: Silence and Listening

When we're burned out, we have solitude because we're no longer able to handle an endless flood of social interactions. Kierkegaard believed that solitude was essential to acquiring oneself. If we're on the phone all day, there is no space for the silence needed to gain self-knowledge. Only if we're silent can we listen and contemplate.

What are we listening to and contemplating? We're listening to our own thoughts and feelings. The art of contemplation is to develop a detachment which allows us to listen to our thoughts and feelings as an observer. If we can't observe how our thoughts trigger emotions, we can't gain insight into where our emotions come from. Once we learn to observe how our thoughts fall into ruts, we can practice new ways of thinking that don't fall into unhelpful ruts.

What happens if we listen to ourselves as observers? What happens if we set aside all the "*shoulds*" that dominated our pre-burnout lives? What happens if we set aside the guilt that we feel for not being able to fulfill all those "*shoulds*"? What happens if set aside everything we feel we're supposed to be doing for others? What happens if we set aside the negative thoughts that trigger the emotions of depression?

What happens is we become more objective about our thoughts and we see how our thoughts create emotions. We come to understand that we can consciously substitute different habits of thought so our thoughts no longer automatically fall into unhelpful ruts.

Like Thoreau, Kierkegaard was a great walker. As noted in the Triage chapter, walking is therapeutic for me and many other burnouts. Walks give us time to reflect while helping to heal our minds and bodies.

We might ponder our path to burnout, and ask if we were in Devil's Pacts we didn't even see. We might contemplate how we weren't fully aware of what we relied on to feel good about ourselves. We might explore our past for memories of what enthused us as young adults. We might imagine being happy with ourselves and our life rather than returning to the struggle of keeping it all glued together.

These are all variations of listening to our thoughts and feelings about ourselves, our lives and our burnout.

We can also ponder the larger contexts of our lives.

Later in life, Merton was interested in Eastern philosophic traditions and published an interpretive translation of the writings of the third century B.C. Chinese Taoist sage, Chuang Tzu (now written as Zhuangzi), *The Way of Chuang Tzu.*

I was first introduced to Taoism in the early 1970s in a university philosophy class taught by the eminent scholar Chung-yuan Chang, translator of the *Tao Te Ching* and author of *Creativity and Taoism*. I mention my decades-long interest in Taoism as context for my interpretation of Merton's writings on Chuang Tzu.

In Merton's reading, the Taoist surrenders *attainment*, not just in the material world of wealth and status but in the spiritual realm. The Taoist isn't trying to become rich and famous or a saint. The goal is to accept one's flaws with humility and forget the self rather than become hyper-self-conscious by constantly comparing oneself to a fixed standard, which is the focus of attainment.

The Taoist is neither seeking attainment (moral purity, wealth, power) or inactive contemplation. The Taoist term *non-action* doesn't mean doing nothing, it means not striving to glorify the prideful self.

Whatever action the Taoist undertakes in *non-action* is aligned with the Tao rather than self-conscious attainment. The Tao manifests in the quiet of the murmuring brook. (This is a phrase from Kierkegaard: *"The presence of the Eternal is like the murmuring of the brook. When you have stopped to listen to it, then it captures you."*)

What does this elusive description of the Tao mean for the burnout? The first line of the *Tao Te Ching* is famously Zenlike: *The Tao that can be spoken of is not the Tao itself.* Nonetheless, as Professor Chang reminded his students, "Even Lao Tzu wrote 5,000 characters about the Tao," and so we must try to describe what it means in practical terms.

We can say the Tao cannot be followed by focusing on attainments that glorify the idealized self we present to the world to win approval.

We can also say that *things open and close themselves and in their own time*. We can decide to resist this opening or closing, or hurry it up or slow it down, but our will cannot reverse the tide. If we try to resist the tide, we will destroy ourselves. In moving with the tide, we are not *making things happen* so much as acting in accordance with what is already happening outside the control of our will.

Our prideful self has great confidence in our power to make things happen no matter what is in our way. This stubborn pride in our own strength refuses to back down because that makes us feel weak. And so we continue fighting the tide until we finally burn out.

Metaphorically, burnout saves us from completely destroying ourselves: we want to continue swimming against the current just to show that we can force things to go the way we want them to go, but our stubborn pride exhausts us and we burn out.

If we try to force something even as it exhausts us, this is not aligning with the tide, it is swimming against the tide. Our prideful self feels that giving up trying to force something is a shameful defeat, and so we swim even harder against the current until we burn out.

We may accept our burnout but try to speed up the recovery. Things not only open and close on their own, *they do so on their own time*. Trying to rush things that can't be rushed is trying to force the current to reverse because we want it to. We can't will everything to follow what we've decided would suit us. We can only be open to swimming with the current rather than against it.

Pride wants to control and hurry everything; humility accepts that things unfold in their own time.

In my experience, we can't help being carried along by the currents of our authentic self and interests. We can resist and swim against these currents, but this wears us down and burns us out.

We have to swim within the current of who we are.

Inevitably, we sometimes bump up against our own limits. If we try to force those limits, we end up burning out. We serve our own interests best by accepting our limits with humility.

We think that once we understand that *things open and close all by themselves and on their own time* that we can then control this to get what we want. But we cannot control what opens and closes. Understanding doesn't give us control; it offers insight and humility.

Earlier in the book I asked you to recall a time when your workload was heavy but you were energized; you slept well and awoke with enthusiasm for the day. That positive energy arose from self-expression and your alignment with what was *opening and closing all by themselves*—swimming with the current rather than against it.

Now compare that to your workload just prior to burning out: didn't it all feel forced? Where was the energizing self-expression and enthusiasm? Those positives had been replaced by drudgery, as everything became an ordeal. We were on a treadmill of exhaustion and depression. We felt distraught, not energized.

We spend a great deal of energy trying to convince ourselves that forcing something is the right thing to do—for our career, to meet the expectations of others, to reach a standard we'd set for ourselves. But all these are focused on externalities: attainments or what others want.

No matter how much we try to convince ourselves that forcing something is the right decision, we can't force ourselves to feel enthusiasm for something that doesn't tap into our true selves rather than add some glitter to the façade we present to others.

In my experience, writing our dreams down upon awakening offers insight into our emotional lives—not what we try to convince ourselves we feel, but what we really feel. If we seek hints about the currents in our lives and what we're forcing, we may gain insight into the sources of our burnout and paths out of burnout.

You may recall my dream about crossing a dry riverbed while seeking a remote jobsite and returning to find a raging river that I could not cross to return to my car and mobile phone. My interpretation is that the car and phone represented my old life that I could not return to. I had no way to communicate this to others (no mobile phone) and no easy way to leave (no car). I was on my own.

I think this is an accurate metaphor for burnout: we can't go back to our former life but we can't communicate this to others. Our will is powerless against the raging river: trying to force our way across the raging river leads to our own destruction.

If we listen to our dreams, they may offer insight into our situation and clarify how we really feel.

Our exploration of silence and listening wouldn't be complete without discussing *listening to others and wanting them to listen to us*. Humans are social animals and we communicate in a variety of ways. Just sitting quietly together can communicate something.

When we're burned out, our ability to interact with others is greatly diminished. We simply don't have the energy required to pay attention to others. We are best served by limiting our interactions to those which nurture us rather than drain us.

Most of us like when others listen to us. In a conversation, each participant is both speaker and audience. In one-sided conversations, one person is mostly the audience for the other person.

It may be that the speaker is dominating the conversation because they're providing important information to the listener. But in many cases, the speaker is repeating memories or complaints and rehashing their woes.

Invoking Kierkegaard's either/or: people are either *solving their problems or they're maintaining their problems* so they can continue getting the purpose and security the problems give them.

Listening to a person reporting their progress on solving problems is being one kind of audience. Listening to a person repeat the same old complaints and woes while they refuse to resolve the sources of their problem is being another kind of audience.

Listening to someone actively solving their problems engages us, as they typically welcome our encouragement, questions and suggestions. Listening to someone repeating their complaints and woes is draining, as they resent our exhaustion with being their passive audience.

They also resist any attempt to direct the conversation toward solving their problems. They repeat all the reasons why their problems are unresolvable: I was wronged, I'm trapped, etc.

Listening to people repeat their woes and why their problems are unresolvable is draining. It isn't helpful or nurturing to the burnout.

Communicating what you're experiencing can be nurturing or draining. Trying to explain burnout to an unsympathetic person is a draining dead-end, as their frustration and tone-deafness isn't helpful.

But the burnout must also be aware that holding forth on the suffering of burnout turns whomever was kind enough to listen to into a silent audience. Repeating the woes of burnout burdens others and doesn't resolve the sources of burnout.

The burnout best serves their own healing by limiting communication to the helpful variety. Solving problems is aided by sharing what we've learned, listening to the helpful ideas of others and expressing gratitude to anyone kind enough to pay attention.

Once the burnout starts feeling better, we are able to extend very valuable empathy and understanding to other burnouts. No one really understands burnout like those who have already experienced burnout.

I would like to share some thoughts on silence and listening that the faithful might find useful. Non-believers may glean something beneficial as well. If this is of no interest, feel free to skip these few paragraphs.

Kierkegaard held that we cannot will faith, we can only will an openness to faith. Like enthusiasm, faith is the equalizer—all can have faith. But we are all different in our degree of faith and how we understand and manifest faith.

To paraphrase Merton: God wants each of us to be ourselves, and in being ourselves we are obeying God and fulfilling His purpose for each of us. We have a duty to be ourselves and to accept this duty positively. We don't have to be perfect to accept God's grace, and our faith doesn't have to be perfect for us to accept God's grace.

Thomas Merton's prayer may speak to those struggling with burnout:

My Lord God,

I have no idea where I am going.

I do not see the road ahead of me.

I cannot know for certain where it will end.

nor do I really know myself,

and the fact that I think I am following your will

does not mean that I am actually doing so.

But I believe that the desire to please you

does in fact please you.

And I hope I have that desire in all that I am doing.

I hope that I will never do anything apart from that desire.

And I know that if I do this you will lead me by the right road,

though I may know nothing about it.

Therefore will I trust you always though

I may seem to be lost and in the shadow of death.

I will not fear, for you are ever with me,

and you will never leave me to face my perils alone.

I'll end this chapter with two thoughts on silence: *Silence is a form of prayer*, and Kierkegaard's poetic invocation of the power of listening: *"The presence of the Eternal is like the murmuring of the brook. When you have stopped to listen to it, then it captures you."*

I have used the word *enthusiasm* as the source of the guiding light within us. The Greek root word means divine inspiration, i.e., God within us. To pursue our enthusiasms can be understood as listening to the divine inspiration within us.

The poet Rumi spoke to this when he wrote: *"From this I understand that what I want also wants me, is looking for me and attracting me. There is a great secret here for anyone who can grasp it."*

Rumi also wrote about silence and listening:
The inspiration you seek
Is already within you.
Be silent and listen.

Chapter Eleven: Life Beyond Burnout

Let's recap. This is my experience. Yours might be very different.

We cling to what we feel we must have even though it no longer works for us, so we burn out. Burnout is an *involuntary intolerance for what no longer works in our lives.*

Burnout is the governor which shuts us down before we self-destruct. It is an involuntary safety mechanism that protects us from damaging ourselves further.

We didn't choose to burn out. We want to heal and advance.

To heal and advance, we must identify the sources of our burnout and eliminate or reduce them.

We can't go on, but we must go on. We will go on.

Burnout is a gift, an opportunity to reassess and renew our lives. The poet Rumi's line summarizes the burnout's opportunity: *"Where there is ruin, there is hope for a treasure."*

Looking beyond burnout, we need a livelihood and a way of life that reflects our enthusiasms and limits the sources of burnout.

If we try to return to the situation that burned us out, we will burn out again. If we pursue options that aren't realistic, we'll remain stuck on Square One or return to it.

Everyone's circumstances are unique, and these goals may have no value to anyone else. These are my life-beyond-burnout goals.

Four Goals

Goal #1: avoid the burnout-recovery-go back to work-burnout cycle. We're not recovering just to go back to what burned us out. We have to make changes in our life.

Goal #2: eliminate or reduce the sources of burnout. What causes *chronic stress*? Open-ended commitments and complexity.

I've already discussed the difference between open-ended and limited commitments. Open-ended commitments lead to open-ended workloads and sacrifices because there's no limit on what's demanded of us whole our control and rewards are limited.

Unpredictability goes hand in hand with open-ended commitments. Unpredictability generates stress. If we're on call for work, every ring of the phone creates anxiety: is my day/evening about to be upended?

If we control our commitments, we can set limits. If others have the power to demand open-ended commitments from us, then we're stuck in the burnout-go back to work-burnout cycle.

Work that is within our control allows us to *do good work while we're at work* without burning out.

Modern life is complex. It's difficult to reduce complexity. Once again, the keys to managing complexity are *control and predictability.* It's less stressful to manage complex things if they're predictable and we control the process.

For example, if we're self-employed, we have to pay estimated taxes, excise taxes, etc. These are predictable kinds of complexity. Other kinds of complexity are open-ended and outside our control, and these complexities don't just add stress, they multiply stress.

Complexity that serves our enthusiasms and that we control is not draining like complexity we don't control. Many projects we do for pleasure are complex (gardening, crafts, music, home improvement, etc.) but the rewards are well worth the effort.

There is only so much we can do to reduce burdensome complexity. Managing people, enterprises, compliance, regulations, etc. is inherently complex. The practical solution is to eliminate sources of complexity entirely by simplifying our life.

Before burnout, this seemed impossible. Now we know it's not just possible but necessary, for burnout radically simplified our life.

Eliminating open-ended commitments and complexities reduces sources of chronic stress and overwork.

Goal #3 is becoming not just a survivor but more adaptable, what author Nassim Taleb calls *antifragile*. In Taleb's words: *"The resilient resists shocks and stays the same; the antifragile gets better."*

Trying to stay the same doesn't work for burnouts because that means keeping what burned us out the same.

By exposing our limits, burnout offers us an opportunity to evolve beyond whatever burned us out by becoming more flexible and adaptable, i.e., more self-reliant. If we become more adaptable, we can modify our lives to avoid getting burned out again.

Taleb titled his book *Antifragile: Things That Gain from Disorder.* By disorder, he doesn't mean chaos; in my view, he's referring to the constant flux of pressures and experimentation that guide Nature, including human cultures and each of us.

When pressures mount, organisms try a variety of new things to find the most successful response. This ability to experiment and select what works and let go of what doesn't is the essence of antifragility.

Part of why we burned out is we tried to keep everything the same even when it no longer worked for us. As the pressure increased, we clung on even harder, until we burned out.

Clinging on to what's no longer working makes us fragile.

Being dependent on one thing leaves us fragile. For example, if our household depends solely on one source of income, if that source is lost the consequences will be severe.

If we have multiple incomes from different sources, the loss of one income will hurt but we can find ways to adapt and survive.

If we rely on an external source for our purpose and self-worth—for example, our job—losing that source is devastating.

 If we draw purpose and self-worth from inner sources and a mix of activities, the loss of one source won't leave us lost and depressed.

In other words, the goal is not to maintain our fragility but to increase our adaptability by expanding our control of our work and life.

Goal #4: Make a realistic assessment of ourselves, our constraints and our options for a livelihood and a way of life. Burnout changed our lives. The essence of antifragility is to expect change and be prepared to adapt to it.

To do this, we need a clear-eyed assessment of our limits and a realistic accounting of our work and financial options. What do we need to change to right-size our work, finances and way of life to the realities of what we can manage without burning out?

Ideal solutions may be out of reach. We need a realistic assessment of our situation to assess what options are within reach.

Taking Care of Ourselves

These generalizations about taking care of ourselves helped me.

One is that burnout limits how much energy is in our tank even after we recover enough to return to work. We can think of this as a bank account with limited funds to invest.

Our limited resources force us to prioritize care to those most in need. In the case of those recovering from burnout, that is ourselves. We no longer have enough energy to stay in situations that drain us.

If we want to help others, we must first help ourselves. We can't give all of ourselves away. If we don't take care of ourselves, we won't be able to help anyone else.

Some of us may need to limit our social interactions to take care of ourselves. Socializing may be too draining.

People who were accustomed to having us as their audience may well be indignant that we're no longer available. But there simply isn't enough in our tank to spend on people and situations that drain us of the energy we need for ourselves.

A second generality is that we're still ourselves. Burnout changed our life, but it doesn't turn us into an entirely different person. For example, I'm still manic-depressive and impatient, just as I was before burnout.

We need to identify what habits of thought added fuel to our burnout, and forge new habits that reduce rather than escalate burnout.

A third generality is our emotional resources may be limited. We may no longer have the reserves to engage others' problems.

If I take on someone's emotional burdens, I haven't removed their burdens. They still have all their problems. All I've done is drain myself. Once I'm drained, I have nothing left for myself or anyone else.

No matter how much we want to help another burnout, we can't fix their burnout. Only they can fix their burnout. As writer Marcel Proust insightfully said, "We don't receive wisdom; we must discover it for ourselves after a journey that no one can take for us or spare us." Burnout is a voyage each of us must take ourselves.

Our intellectual resources may also have limits. The most troubling aspects of my burnout were the sharp increase in forgetfulness, the decline in my concentration and the decay in my judgement. I made errors while driving that were uncharacteristic of my pre-burnout life. I also made poor financial decisions and uncharacteristic mistakes in small building projects that bother me to this day.

Ignoring these constraints leads to poor results.

Navigating our emergence from burnout isn't a single step, it is a dynamic process involving all aspects of ourselves and our lives. We must learn to take care of ourselves as the first essential step.

Tapping Our Enthusiasms

I've spent a lot of time on the need to develop new ways of feeling good about ourselves that tap our authentic self and enthusiasms.

For example, those of us who defined ourselves as *hard workers* may need to change our identity to *doing good work*. Instead of exploiting ourselves to prove how hard we work, we can cut our work schedule and focus on *doing good work while we're at work*. Then we go home. Our identity shifts from being self-exploiting *hard workers* to doing *good work while we're at work*.

With this inner change, we eliminate one inner source of burnout: being our own exploitive boss.

Those of us who defined ourselves as helpers may need to change our identity from *helper* to *aiding others in ways that express our enthusiasms.*

For example, I am not a trained therapist. Listening to other's emotional, career or relationship problems is extremely draining because this is not my skill or enthusiasm.

Carpentry and building are enthusiasms of mine. I was a builder for five years and my business partner and I built dozens of custom homes, a 43-unit subdivision and a large commercial building.

When someone asks for my help with a carpentry project, I get something out of helping them: I get to express one of my enthusiasms.

When someone asks me to edit their research paper or make suggestions on their book draft, I am happy to help because writing is one of my enthusiasms. I can help others with their carpentry and writing projects but I can't resolve their emotional, career and relationship problems.

Identifying Our Sources of Burnout

In my view, those of us hacking our way out of the jungle of burnout must identify every source of our burnout and lay out a new way of living that eliminates or strictly limits each source.

As an example, here is my list of burnout sources I needed to eliminate or drastically limit. This is my list; yours will be different.

A business that became increasingly complex, demanding and burdensome. The workload never slackened, it only increased.

A property that needed a complete re-do of all the work we'd done 25 years ago: new paint and other major maintenance that comes with buildings that are 60+ years old.

Local regulations that constantly increased compliance, paperwork and costs such as business license fees.

Increasing urban decay and insecurity (permanent homeless encampments a block away, etc.) and the displacement by cookie-cutter corporate chains of small businesses that had given the town its unique character: *Small is beautiful, Big is ugly.*

A feeling that I'd wrung every drop of value from the locale and was done with it.

A loss of fulfillment from running the business and interacting with customers/clients.

Physical limits on my energy as I entered my mid-60s.

Being constantly drained by others' unresolvable problems.

Extreme housing costs meant we could never own more than a postage stamp of land.

Recall that the goal is to eliminate destructive stressors so we regain our capacity to enjoy life, do good work and help those we care about.

The real-world solution was to sell our business and property and move to a new locale without all the costs and stressors of the place we left.

This required a difficult decision process as my spouse did not want to sell or move. This conflict was only resolved when I burned out. The burden of running the business by herself burned her out within six months. Only then was she able to let go.

We'd been scouting neighborhoods and homes in the new locale, so when a property with the kind of yard, older traditional-style home and location we'd wanted came on the market, we bought it for a fraction of what the property would have cost in the locale we left.

The new locale lacks the extreme wealth inequality and urban decay (the two are related) of the locale we left, and we have family and friends here.

Internally, the solution was to let go of feeling that I needed to be an audience for everyone who wanted to unburden themselves and to understand that feeling guilty about setting limits was not helpful.

These solutions eliminated or greatly reduced the sources of stress.

Just as it took years of stress to push us over the cliff into burnout, advancing out of burnout may also take years.

Four years after I hit bottom, I'm still learning about my post-burnout self and experience. Only recently did I come to understand the difference between engaging those who cling to their problems and those who are sincerely trying to solve their problems. Pouring our heart and soul into trying to help those who have no interest in actually changing is a dead-end: nothing we say or do will make a difference.

Everyone is better off if we invest our limited energy in someone who does want to change: ourselves.

Chronic stress dulls our awareness. We may not even be aware of aspects of our lives that wear us down.

It took a long time to understand how the urban ugliness of my former locale was a source of chronic negativity. In contrast, working in my productive yard that's brimming with beauty and good things to eat is a continual source of inspiration, satisfaction and joy.

The lack of control also wears us down. I had no control over the ugliness around me in my old locale. There was nothing I could do about soaring fees, expanding homeless encampments, crime and the decline of local businesses.

In contrast, I Have a lot control over our yard: we've planted fruit trees and vegetable gardens, removed piles of unsightly rocks, etc.

We also had little control over the business environment. Our choice was put up with the increasingly burdensome bureaucracy, taxes and other expenses or leave.

In contrast, my writing business is largely within my control. I scaled back my workload to what I could sustain. My spouse has a scaled-down, low-key, limited version of our previous business as a source of fulfilling part-time work that generates a modest income.

This enterprise has a fraction of the old business's revenues, expenses, work, stress and income. It has no sources of toxic chronic stress and is within our control.

Gaining Control of Our Life

In my experience, having control of one's life, skills, assets, enterprises and locale is priceless. Skills, assets, enterprises and properties all have price tags, but control of one's life has no price because it's irreplaceable. There is no substitute for control of one's life.

Jobs over which we have little control are stressful. Ways of living that we have little control over are also stressful. The more we control, the greater our potential to weed out sources of destructive stress.

If we have little control, we're stuck with the consequences of others' decisions. We have to accept what's happening to us whether it works for us or not.

The burnout has a great advantage: burnout forced us to let go of whatever we were clinging to. We have no choice; we have to let go. As terrible as this may feel at the time, it is immensely freeing.

Having control is even more important for those emerging from burnout because we need to limit the stressors that cause burnout. The less we control, the harder this becomes. The more we control, the easier it becomes.

It's constructive to separate what we control from what we don't control.

We don't control what assets will be worth or the financial system. We do control how much debt we owe. We control how much of our income goes to superfluous consumption and how much we waste. We control what property we own and where we own it.

The less we need for a good life, the lower our stress.

What we're discussing here are tradeoffs.

In my experience, agency—the power to change our lives—is worth more than money. Gaining control and maintaining control requires tradeoffs, because all the things we're programmed to believe are the sources of happiness—wealth, status, etc.—require giving power to others and to systems beyond our control.

Making tradeoffs is part of life. The question is: at what cost to ourselves and our health? We burned out because we accepted toxic stress as the price of whatever we thought was valuable.

Burnout forces us to reconsider what's truly valuable. We discover our health is more valuable than anything else because once burnout breaks our health, we lose everything.

We discover agency is more valuable than success because we need agency to weed out sources of toxic stress.

In my experience, emerging from burnout requires understanding that the time where we could trade our health for things that cause toxic stress are over. Whatever's left that doesn't cause toxic stress is what we have to work with.

It may look like a lot less to those on the outside, but to the burnout, recovering our health is all that really counts. Since control of our lives is necessary to recover our health, agency counts, too.

Whatever has to be sacrificed to maintain our self-reliance, agency and health, so be it.

This is the blessing of burnout: we can no longer destroy ourselves because burnout shuts down the tradeoffs that sacrificed our health.

Burnout keeps us honest. We can't trade one source of toxic stress for another source of toxic stress and tell ourselves this is an improvement.

We all want to be productive and useful, valued for our contributions and appreciated as honest, fair-minded, trustworthy individuals. We all want to earn self-respect.

The goal is to find ways to become productive that don't require sacrificing our agency and health. This requires tradeoffs.

Where We Are Now

I'll conclude this account of my experience of burnout by answering the question, where are we now, almost four years after we burned out?

Neither my spouse nor I can say we've gone back to where we were four years ago. We've changed. We can no longer work that hard or carry that much stress, nor do we want to.

Does that mean we're still burned out?

I understand why comparing workloads before and after burnout is the measure many use to assess whether we've recovered. From my perspective, a return to the work and stress that burned us out isn't a success, it's a failure, for it means we learned very little.

If burnout is a life-changing experience rather than just a bump in the road, the more meaningful question is: do we have *a good life* that fits our energy and enthusiasms?

For me, the main lesson of burnout is that if our life doesn't align with our energy and enthusiasms, something breaks. If we cling to what's breaking us, we burn out. Once we burn out, we can't cling on. Burnout gives us an opportunity to align our life with *who we are* right now.

Burning out in our 60s when age saps our middle-age energy is different from burning out in our 20s or 30s. It's impossible for me to assess how much of the decline in my energy is the result of aging or burnout, because both occurred at the same time.

I attribute the collapse of my tolerance for sources of stress to burnout. I avoid media reports of distant traumas and individuals' traumas over which I have no control.

While I understand why some might view this as fragility and/or indifference, I view it as a positive recognition that there is no gain in burdening myself with sources of stress that I can't influence.

I think it a wiser use of my scarce time and energy to solve whatever problems I can influence. This requires prioritizing taking care of myself first so I have some energy to devote to others.

One duty that added to our overwork was the need to care for my elderly mother-in-law. There was no way to do that and run an increasingly burdensome business.

The solution boiled down to selling out and buying a house where she could live with us and still maintain her own independence. This took several years to accomplish.

I need more time alone now to restore my ability to pay attention to others. The solitude of working in the yard is restorative, as is the boundless beauty of the trees, plants and gardens.

Much of our built world is hopelessly ugly, and this drains us in ways few recognize. Nature restores us.

Am I still burned out? The question assumes that returning to our pre-burnout life is the goal. Burnout changes our understanding of a good life. I can't go back to the unhappiness of toxic stress, nor do I want to. What's important is our way of life fits our modest energy levels and enables us to fulfill our duties and enthusiasms.

Is there a point where I can say, "I'm no longer burned out"? I don't know. It may remain unknowable for the rest of my life. I don't think the goal is to be able to say "I'm no longer burned out." I think the goal is to acquire yourself and express your authentic self in fulfilling your duties and enthusiasms.

For me, burnout, like life, is a learning process. I'm still learning.

This is my experience. I hope it adds something, however modest, to your understanding of burnout and life.

Charles Hugh Smith

Made in the USA
Las Vegas, NV
16 July 2022